Published in the United States and its territories and Canada by
HAMMOND WORLD ATLAS CORPORATION
Part of the Langenscheidt Publishing Group

36-36 33rd Street, Long Island City, NY 11106

EXECUTIVE EDITOR: Nel Yomtov

EDITOR: Kevin Somers

Produced for Hammond World Atlas Corporation by

MOSELEY ROAD INC.

129 MAIN STREET

IRVINGTON, NY 10533

WWW.MOSELEYROAD.COM

MOSELEY ROAD INC.

PUBLISHER Sean Moore

ART DIRECTORS Brian MacMullen, Gus Yoo

EDITORIAL DIRECTOR Lisa Purcell

EDITOR Ward Calhoun

PHOTO RESEARCHER Ben DeWalt

DESIGNER Joanne Flynn

CARTOGRAPHY Neil Dvorak

EDITORIAL ASSISTANTS Rachael Lanicci, Natalie Rivera

COVER DESIGN Linda Kosarin

Printed and bound in Canada

ISBN-13: 978-0843-718966

HAMMOND UNDERCOVER™

SPACE

LORI BAIRD

HAMMOND World Atlas
Part of the Langenscheidt Publishing Group

Contents

What is Space?

The National Aeronautics and Space Administration (NASA) tells us that "space" is the area beyond our atmosphere where stars, moons, planets, and other bodies are found. It's difficult to say exactly where space begins, because there are no distinct boundaries between the layers of the atmosphere.

Gases in the atmosphere disperse wavelengths of blue light that give Earth what appears from space to be a glowing blue outer ring.

Earth's Atmosphere

Earth is surrounded by several layers of gas, mostly nitrogen and oxygen. Combined, these gas layers are known as our atmosphere. The atmosphere gives Earth its weather and climate and protects it from the harmful effects of the sun. Here's a guide to the atmospheric layers that separate us from space.

Troposphere

• Extends from Earth's surface to an altitude of about 10 miles
• Commercial airliners fly in the troposphere. At present, the highest a commercial jet can fly is 41,000 feet.
• Earth's weather occurs in the troposphere.
• Average temperature decreases as altitude increases in the troposphere.
• Nearest Earth, the atmosphere is dense and rich in oxygen. It becomes increasingly thin as altitude is gained.
• Most life on Earth occurs at altitudes of less than 3 miles. Above that, decreased oxygen in the air makes breathing difficult.

Stratosphere

• Occurs from about 10 miles to 30 miles
• The ozone layer is located in the stratosphere. Ozone is a type of oxygen. The layer it forms in the upper stratosphere absorbs and protects us from the sun's dangerous ultraviolet radiation.
• Temperatures increase with altitude in the stratosphere, because the ozone layer absorbs the sun's radiation and heat.
• The stratosphere is very dry. Very few if any clouds are found there.
• When objects or particles—gases and debris from volcanic eruptions or exhaust from rocket launches, for instance—enter the stratosphere, they can remain there for months or years.

Mesosphere

• Occurs from about 30 miles to about 53 miles above Earth
• The air here is very thin, but it is still thick enough to burn up meteoroids.
• This layer of the atmosphere is quite cold, with temperatures as low as –130°F.

Thermosphere

- Occurs from altitudes of about 53 miles to 370 miles or more
- Also known as the upper atmosphere
- The International Space Station, space shuttles, and some weather and photo satellites orbit in this layer.
- As might be guessed from its name—*thermo* is Greek for "heat"—the thermosphere is the hottest layer, because it absorbs so much solar radiation. Temperatures here increase with altitude and can reach 2,730°F or more.

Exosphere

- Stretches from the end of the thermosphere to 5,500 miles, where it gives way to outer space
- Composed of hydrogen and helium, but in very low densities
- Some military, spy, and navigation satellites orbit in this layer of the atmosphere.

DID YOU KNOW?

Look at any photograph of the moon, and you'll see that its surface is covered with craters. These craters were caused by meteor strikes. Now look at the land around you. No craters, right? It's not that we've been luckier than the moon. Earth has seen just as many meteors as the moon. But most of them burn up in our atmosphere before ever reaching Earth. The moon has no atmosphere and therefore has no protective layer.

Earth's atmosphere consists of five basic layers.

EXOSPHERE

THERMOSPHERE

MESOSPHERE

STRATOSPHERE

TROPOSPHERE

370–5,500 MILES

53–370 MILES

30–53 MILES

10–30 MILES

4–10 MILES

Stars and Planets

For thousands and thousands of years, humans did not understand that Earth was part of a much larger "community" of other planets, moons, a sun—a galaxy. For a long while, people believed that Earth was the center of the solar system. It wasn't until the sixteenth century that a Polish astronomer—Nicolaus Copernicus (1473-1543)—was able to prove scientifically that the sun was the center of our solar system. That development is considered to have been the beginning of modern astronomy. Over time, this science helped us to imagine and build tools and equipment that would allow us to learn more about, and eventually travel to, space.

The Milky Way

Gaze into the sky on a clear night, and if it is dark enough where you are, you will see it: a broad band of light that stretches across the sky. That is the Milky Way, the galactic home of the planet Earth and our entire solar system.

If you could look at the Milky Way from the side, you would see that it is shaped like a disk with a bulge in the center.

Our home: the amazing Milky Way galaxy

THE MILKY WAY

Size: 100,000 light-years in diameter, 1,000 light-years thick

Age: 13 billion years, as old as the universe

Composition: Dust, gas, and more than 200 billion stars

Where did it get its name?
Tradition has it that the Milky Way was named for a Greek myth, in which the goddess Hera spills milk and it sprays across the sky.

WHAT ARE LIGHT-YEARS?

Space is so vast that usual measurements—miles and kilometers—are not useful. To measure distances in space, scientists use a unit called the "light-year." One light-year is equal to the distance light travels in one year. Light travels at a speed of 186,411 miles per second, or 6.2 trillion kilometers in a year.

THE SUN

Our sun is located in one of the galaxy's spiraling arms.

STARGAZING

CONSTELLATIONS ARE GROUPS of stars and planets that seem to form specific shapes—such as animals or objects—when seen from Earth. Ancient civilizations created these groupings as a way of helping them remember the stars and their locations.

In 1925, the International Astronomical Union created an official list of 88 recognized constellations. Among the constellations that are easiest to find in the night sky are Orion, the hunter; Ursa Major, or the Big Dipper; Ursa Minor, or the Little Dipper; and Cassiopeia.

From above, the Milky Way looks like a spinning pinwheel. For that reason, it is called a spiral galaxy. In addition to spiral galaxies, two other kinds of galaxies are found in the universe.

Elliptical galaxies are football shaped. Irregular galaxies don't fall into any one kind of shape.

The youngest and brightest stars in the Milky Way are in the bulging area at the center of the disk. The oldest stars in the galaxy, along with dust and gases, are found in the spherical halo that surrounds the disk. The disk itself is where most of the stars are found, including our own sun.

Our solar system sits 26,000 light-years from the center of the Milky Way galaxy, on one of the spiraling "arms" at its outer edge, called the Orion Arm.

Constellation charts, like the one above, and sky maps are used to locate stars, constellations, and other objects in the sky for certain dates, times, and observing locations.

STAR LIGHT, STAR BRIGHT

Our sun is not the brightest star in the universe. It seems so bright to us because the sun is the closest star to Earth: only 92,955,820 miles away. Sounds like a lot, but that is only 8.3 light minutes away. The brightest known star in our universe is Sirius. In fact, it's about 25 times brighter than our sun! But because Sirius is so far away—8.6 light-years—it is visible to us only at night, but even then it is the brightest star in the night sky. Sirius can be seen as part of the constellation Canis Major, or the "Big Dog," which is near Orion.

The Solar System

THE SUN
Closest star to Earth (92.96 million miles); largest object in our solar system (radius of 864,400 miles), 109 times larger than Earth; sphere of gases, mostly hydrogen and helium; temperature ranges from 27,000,000°F at its core to 10,000°F on its surface.

EARTH
Third (92.95 million miles) from the sun; only planet with liquid water; unique atmosphere of mostly nitrogen and oxygen protects planet from the sun's dangerous rays and meteors; fifth largest planet, radius of about 3,963 miles; one day is 23 hours, 56 minutes; one year is 365 days, 6 hours, and 16 minutes.

MARS
Fourth (141.63 million miles) from the sun; reddish-brown dust on its surface gives it its nickname "Red Planet"; thin atmosphere of carbon dioxide; arid, rocky; evidence of ice, but no signs of life in polar ice caps; about half the size of Earth, radius of about 2,111 miles; one day equal to 24 hours, 37 minutes; one year equal to about 687 Earth days.

URANUS
Seventh (1,783 million miles) from the sun; a "gas" planet, comprised mostly of hydrogen and helium; four times larger than Earth, radius of 15,882 miles; methane in atmosphere cause its blue-green color; tilts so much that it rotates on its side; coldest planet; temperature hovers at about −355°F; one year equal to 84 Earth years; one day just over 17 hours.

SATURN
Sixth (885.90 million miles) from the sun; a "gas" planet, composed primarily of hydrogen and helium; nearly nine times larger than Earth, radius of 37,449 miles; dust, rock, and ice make up rings; some of the pieces are small and dustlike, others are up to a half mile across; one year on Saturn is equal to 29.5 Earth years; one day lasts for 10.5 hours.

JUPITER
Fifth (483.68 million miles) from the sun; radius of 44,423 miles; largest planet in solar system, 11 times larger than Earth; a "gas" planet, composed almost entirely of hydrogen and helium; planet's stripes caused by strong east–west winds in upper atmosphere; "Great Red Spot" is a giant spinning storm; average temperature is −234°F; one day is 10 hours; one year equal to 4,331 Earth days.

MERCURY
First (35.98 million miles) from the sun; not the hottest planet; daytime temperatures can reach 800°F; thin atmosphere cannot retain the sun's heat, so nighttime temperatures plunge to −279°F; rocky, cratered terrain; radius of 1,516 miles, about a third the size of Earth; one day equal to 58.65 Earth days; one year is about 88 Earth days.

VENUS
Second (67.23 million miles) from the sun; brightest object in the night sky; about the same size as Earth, radius of 3,760 miles; mountainous terrain with plains and craters; thick atmosphere of carbon dioxide and sulfuric acid traps the sun's heat, making it the hottest planet; temperatures reach 880°F; rotates from east to west on its axis; sun rises in the west and sets in the east; Venusian day (243 Earth days) is longer than its year (225 Earth days).

Our solar system is made up of the eight planets as well as the hundreds of moons and thousands of other objects, including asteroids, comets, and meteoroids, that travel around our sun. Ours is not the only solar system in the Milky Way. Scientists have detected about 70 others, but there may be even more.

What's What in the Solar System

Our solar system is home to asteroids, meteoroids, meteors, and meteorites. What's the difference among them?

Asteroids are large rocks. Some are just a few feet in size, but other asteroids are several hundred miles across. Most of the asteroids in our solar system are found circling the sun in an area between the orbits of Mars and Jupiter called the "asteroid belt."

Rocks and other space debris that are smaller than .62 miles are called meteoroids. When a meteoroid enters our atmosphere and burns up, it creates a flash of light called a shooting star, or a meteor.

If a meteoroid does not burn up in our atmosphere but instead lands on Earth, it's called a meteorite. Most meteorites are tiny, but some have weighed as much as 220 pounds.

Comets are asteroids that are covered with dust and ice. When the comet gets close to the sun in its orbit, some of the ice melts and winds push the melted ice away from the comet, forming its tail.

NEPTUNE

Eighth (2,795 million miles) from the sun; "gas" planet composed of hydrogen, helium, and methane—which gives it its blue color; radius of 15,388 miles, four times larger than Earth; Great Dark Spot is an enormous storm; solar system's strongest winds found here; one year is equal to 165 Earth years; one day is just over 16 hours.

WHAT ABOUT PLUTO?

In 2006, Pluto was "demoted" from a planet to a dwarf planet by the International Astronomical Union. Why? Because unlike other planets, Pluto does not "clear the neighborhood around its orbit." In other words, Pluto shares its orbit with other objects in space.

PLANETARY MOVEMENTS

A PLANET MOVES in two ways. It revolves around the sun in an oval path called an orbit and at the same time it rotates around an imaginary line running from its north to south pole. That line is called the axis.

A year on any planet is the amount of time it takes to revolve once around the sun; Earth revolves around the sun every 365.25 days. A day is the amount of time it takes to make one full rotation on its axis. For Earth, that is about 24 hours.

The Night Sky

The heavens have always fascinated humankind—but of course, in the beginning, people didn't understand space and our place in it as well as we do now. Even though humans began to study the stars and planets in about 3000 BCE, accurate understanding didn't come for centuries: up until the mid-1400s CE, for instance, many people still believed that Earth was the center of the universe. Some of the other assumptions people made about the stars and planets were just as off base. But many of the theories, assumptions, and inventions of those who came before us were surprisingly advanced.

Now Cover Your Right Eye

The Big Dipper is one of the most recognizable constellations in the Northern Hemisphere. The "handle" of the Dipper is made up of five stars: Alkaid, Mizar, Alcor, Alioth, and Megrez. Below, you'll see that Mizar and Alcor are very close together. In fact, they're so near to each other that, if your eyesight is less than perfect, they can appear to be just one star.

Cultures, including the Persians in the thirteenth century, knew that. In fact, they incorporated the stars in ancient eye tests! A fourteenth-century Arab writer referred to the two stars as *Al Sadak,* which translates to "the riddle."

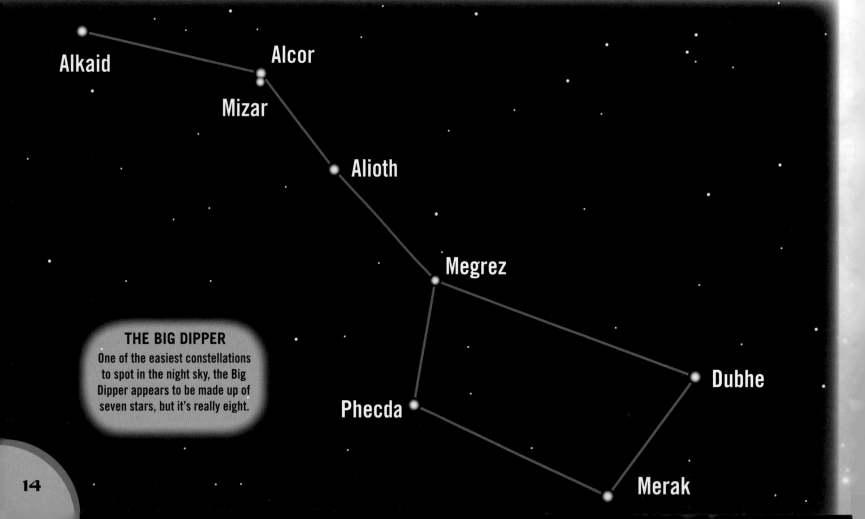

Alkaid

Alcor

Mizar

Alioth

Megrez

Dubhe

THE BIG DIPPER
One of the easiest constellations to spot in the night sky, the Big Dipper appears to be made up of seven stars, but it's really eight.

Phecda

Merak

ASTROLOGICAL SIGNS

Constellation	Symbol	Name/Dates	Constellation	Symbol	Name/Dates
		Aries March 21–April 19			**Libra** September 23–October 23
		Taurus April 20–May 20			**Scorpio** October 24–November 21
		Gemini May 21–June 21			**Sagittarius** November 22–December 21
		Cancer June 22–July 22			**Capricorn** December 22–January 19
		Leo July 23–August 22			**Aquarius** January 20–February 18
		Virgo August 23–September 22			**Pisces** February 19–March 20

Whether you believe in astrology or not, everyone has an astrological sign that corresponds with his or her birthday.

WHATS YOUR SIGN?

FOR MUCH OF HISTORY, astronomy (the scientific study of objects in outer space and the universe) and astrology (the study of horoscopes and the belief that the positions of the planets can affect people and predict events) were closely linked. In fact, some of history's most famous astronomers—Johannes Kepler (1571–1630) and Galileo (1564–1642), for instance—were practitioners of astrology!

It wasn't until about 400 years ago the two became separate. Isaac Newton (1642–1727)—one of history's most influential physicists and mathematicians—was among the first scientists to reject astrology and to rely on observational science.

Among his many contributions to science, Sir Isaac Newton invented the first practical reflecting telescope—a telescope using mirrors to capture an image—in 1669.

THE PROS AREN'T THE ONLY ONES WHO KNOW

The Hale-Bopp comet

AMATEUR ASTRONOMERS HAVE also contributed to our knowledge of space for centuries.

Thomas Bopp (b. 1949) was a co-discoverer of the Hale-Bopp comet, in 1995. His day job? He managed a construction materials factory.

Leslie Peltier (1900–1980) was a high school dropout who later worked as a draftsman. He was also recognized as one of the world's most accomplished amateur astronomers, having discovered 12 comets and two novae during his life.

Will Hay (1888–1949) was a popular British comic actor who starred in 19 films in the thirties and forties. As an astronomy hobbyist, Hay also discovered a large white spot—20,000 miles across—on Saturn, in 1933.

Humans in Space

Humans dreamed about space travel for centuries before it became a real possibility. One of the first mentions of space travel occurs in an ancient Sanskrit poem called the *Ramayana*. In that story, written sometime after 300 BCE, mythical aircraft called Vimana travel to the moon.

In reality, the quest to put humans into space required the work of many different people (and sometimes animals) in several different countries. Some worked in teams, others in isolation. The road was long and often dangerous. But by the end of the twentieth century, not only had a human walked on the moon, but also entire crews of astronauts and scientists had lived and worked in space.

Rockets

Long before rockets were used to send people and equipment into space, they were employed in warfare. The earliest rockets—projectiles filled with shrapnel and propelled by gunpowder—date to 1232. And although weaponry would continue to be their main use through the years, rockets were also used for purposes ranging from powering fireworks displays to launching whale harpoons.

The idea that rocketry could be applied to space travel was first considered seriously from a scientific standpoint in the early twentieth century. The groundwork was laid by three men: a Russian, an American, and a German.

Fueling the Imagination

In 1903, a Russian scientist and school-teacher named Konstantin Tsiolkovsky (1857–1935) developed theories about fueling rockets with liquid propellants—and how that would allow rockets to escape Earth's gravitational field. Considered a pioneer of astronautics, or the science of spaceflight, Tsiolkovsky was partially inspired by the very first science fiction novel, *From the Earth to the Moon*, by Jules Verne. Published in 1865, the book is about a space capsule that is launched from a rocket and lands on the moon.

Oops!

Today, Robert H. Goddard (1882–1945) is universally recognized as the father of modern rocket propulsion. In 1926, he launched the first liquid-fueled rocket—an event that NASA calls as important as the Wright brothers' first airplane flight.

But in 1919, Goddard published a scientific paper in which he speculated that a rocket—if it were large enough and was using the right kind of fuel—could reach the moon. The *New York Times*, in a January 1920 editorial, made fun of Goddard, saying that he "seems to lack the knowledge ladled out daily in high schools." Of course, that editorial was incorrect. In its defense, the paper did apologize for the error—nearly 70 years later, on July 17, 1969—as *Apollo 11* was on its way to the moon.

Designed by inventor William Congreve in 1804, this early rocket was used by the British military and could travel up to 2 miles.

In 1919, Robert Goddard outlined his ideas about the potential of rockets in a paper entitled, "A Method of Reaching Extreme Altitudes."

An Atlas V rocket carrying a Mars exploration spacecraft launches from Cape Canaveral, Florida, on August 12, 2005.

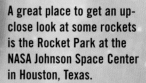

A great place to get an up-close look at some rockets is the Rocket Park at the NASA Johnson Space Center in Houston, Texas.

THE PATH TO IMMORTALITY

A THIRD MAN, Dr. Hermann Oberth (1894–1989), played an enormous role in the development of space rocketry. A German physicist, Oberth was convinced from the start that space travel was possible and, in 1923, published a book about the subject. Due only to a lack of funding, Oberth was never able to transform his theories into a functioning rocket engine, but he did inspire amateur scientists around the world to create rocket societies. Perhaps even more impressive, the creators of the *Star Trek* series named a class of starships after him: the Oberth Class.

SATURN V
The famous Saturn V moon landing rocket was developed at the Marshall Space Flight Center in Huntsville, Alabama.

A Saturn V rocket powers the *Apollo 11* moon landing mission from the Kennedy Space Center in Florida on July 16, 1969.

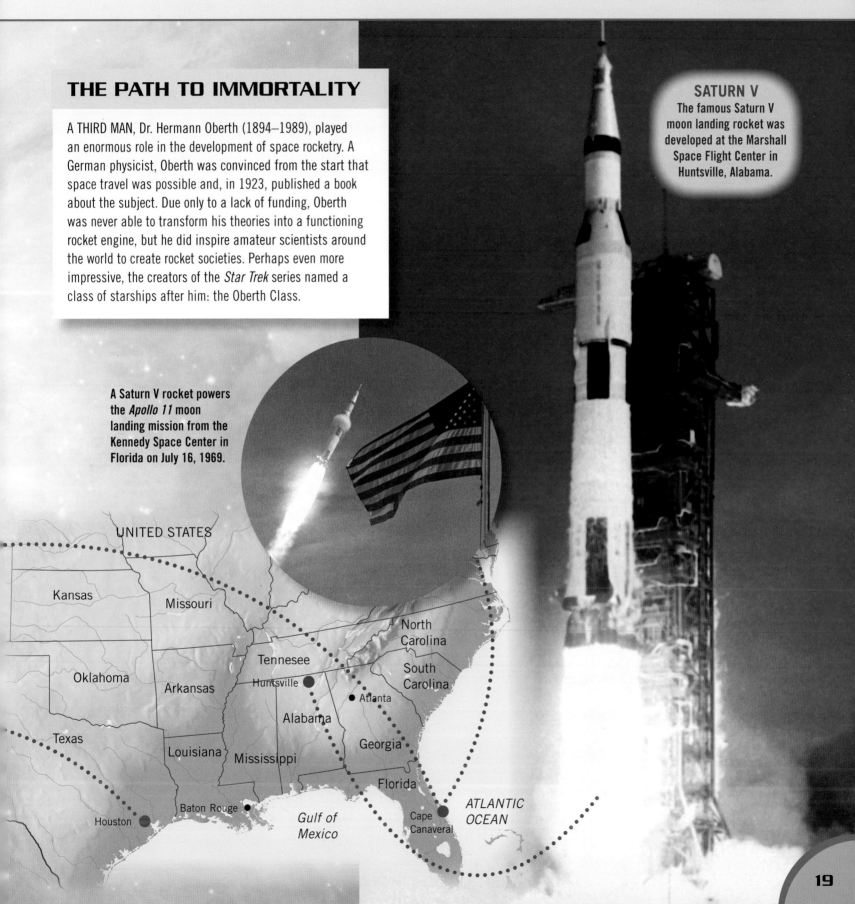

UNITED STATES

Kansas
Missouri
North Carolina
Tennesee
South Carolina
Oklahoma
Arkansas
Huntsville
Atlanta
Alabama
Texas
Georgia
Louisiana
Mississippi
Florida
Baton Rouge
Gulf of Mexico
Cape Canaveral
ATLANTIC OCEAN
Houston

The Birth of NASA

America had long been fascinated with space, but it wasn't until 1915 that the United States government took its first steps toward exploring this final frontier. In that year, Congress created the National Advisory Committee for Aeronautics (NACA). NACA's job was to increase understanding about aeronautics in general and find ways to make flight safer. Most important to space travel, NACA worked with the air force to research and design supersonic aircraft: planes that could fly faster than the speed of sound, or about 761 miles per hour. On October 14, 1947, test pilot Chuck Yeager (b. 1923) did just that in the Bell X-1 rocket plane.

Cold War Catalyst

Further fueling interests in space and aeronautics was the so-called Cold War that developed between the United States and

NACA's humble headquarters were based at the Langley Research Center in Hampton, Virginia.

NASA Centers and Facilities Throughout the United States of America

1	Amnes Research Center- Mottfield, Caliornia	9	Kennedy Space Center- Orlando, Florida
2	Dryden Flight Research Center- Edwards, California	10	Langley Research Center- Hampton, Virginia
3	Glenn Research Center- Cleveland, Ohio	11	Marshall Space Flight Center- Huntsville, Alabama
4	Goddard Space Flight Center- Greenbelt, Maryland	12	NASA Headquarters- Washington, D.C.
5	Goddard Institute of Space Studies- New York, New York	13	NASA Shared Services Center- Stennis, Mississippi
6	IV and V Facility- Fairmont, West Virginia	14	Stennis Space Center- Stennis, Mississippi
7	Jet Propulsion Laboratory- Pasadena, California	15	Wallops Flight Facility- Wallops Island, Virginia
8	Johnson Space Center- Houston, Texas	16	White Sands Test Facility- Las Cruces, New Mexico

the Soviet Union in the aftermath of World War II. As democracy and communism slugged it out on the world stage, both countries engaged in an "anything you can do, I can do better" competition that was perhaps best illustrated by their respective desires to explore space. So, when the Soviets launched a satellite called *Sputnik* in October 1957, the United States scrambled to catch up to its bitter rival.

A Space Agency

On July 29, 1958, President Dwight D. Eisenhower (1890–1969) signed legislation creating the National Aeronautic and Space Administration (NASA). The agency quickly incorporated several other aeronautical organizations and laboratories into its operation and was up and running on October 1, 1958.

NASA scientists had little margin for error. The Soviets early success was an embarrassment to the United States. NASA's mission was to get those rockets into space.

The Kennedy Space Center is a popular tourist destination near Orlando, Florida.

NASA's official logo has four distinct elements: the shape is meant to represent a planet, the stars are space, and the red "V" shape is an airplane wing that is being orbited by a spaceship.

The Race to Space

When the Soviet Union launched the world's first satellite, *Sputnik*, on October 4, 1957, it wasn't exactly the most impressive-looking piece of machinery. In fact, it might best be described as resembling either a giant silver spider or a 184-pound beach ball with legs. Accompanying its simple physical appearance, the satellite itself wasn't designed to do much except orbit around Earth and emit a beeping signal. Nevertheless, *Sputnik*'s launch caught the United States—which had planned to launch its own satellite that year—completely off guard and sparked the space race.

While the United States was still coming to grips with the significance of *Sputnik*, the Soviets launched a second satellite on November 3, 1957. *Sputnik 2* differed from its predecessor in that it was more of a cone-shaped capsule and contained a compartment used to carry the first live cargo into orbit, a dog named Laika. Once again, Russia had beat America to the punch.

A scientist makes some final adjustments to *Sputnik*.

Sputnik was fitted with four antennas that helped transmit a beeping signal back to Earth.

DID YOU KNOW?

The launching of both *Sputnik* satellites and *Explorer 1* were part of a scientific celebration known as the International Geophysical Year (IGY). Spanning from July 1957 to December 1958, IGY invited scientists from around the world to participate in a wide range of experiments and studies on such things as the earth's climate, its oceans, and its atmosphere.

Success!

The United States officially entered the space race on January 31, 1958, with the launch of the *Explorer 1* satellite. Once in orbit, the 80-inch-long, 31-pound satellite circled Earth at a rate of around 12½ orbits per day—for nearly 12 years. It reentered Earth's atmosphere, where it burned up, on March 31, 1970.

A Jupiter-C rocket successfully launches the *Explorer 1* satellite into space from Cape Canaveral, Florida, on January 31, 1958.

The *Vanguard* rocket only got a few feet off the ground before losing thrust and exploding on the launch pad.

FLOPNIK!

IN ITS RUSH to keep pace with the Soviets, the United States—despite the concerns of engineers who felt that the project was not yet ready—attempted to launch its own small satellite into orbit: *Vanguard TV3*. On December 6, 1957, the *Vanguard* rocket carrying the satellite was launched. But after rising only about 4 feet into the air, the rocket sank again and exploded. Texas senator and future president of the United States, Lyndon Johnson, went so far as to call the mishap the "most humiliating failure in America's history." Newspapers around the country used less dignified language, referring to the failed launch as "Flopnik," "Kaputnik," and "Stayputnik."

Animals in Space

Decades before the first human flew into space, agencies from countries including France, Russia, and the United States launched animals on missiles and rockets. They wanted to know whether space travel was safe. How it would affect living creatures? More recently, animals have been used as parts of experiments designed to test the effects of prolonged space travel, weightlessness, and exposure to radiation on biological functions.

Ham the Astrochimp suits up for his mission aboard a Mercury rocket. He is sitting on the edge of his "biopack" space couch.

Space Menagerie
Scientists have sent all sorts of animals into space over the years . . . some we've never even heard of!

ABLE AND BAKER

Able, a 7-pound female rhesus monkey, and Baker, a 1-pound female spider monkey, made history on May 28, 1959, aboard a giant Jupiter rocket. The monkeys flew 360 miles high and were recovered safe and sound. Sadly, Able died four days later from a reaction to anesthesia. But Baker lived to a grand old age, living in a zoo until 1984.

"Miss" Baker, as her handlers called this little squirrel monkey, poses on a model of a Jupiter rocket—the kind of rocket she rode into space.

Amphibians
Bullfrogs, Japanese tree frogs, and newts have all seen the inside of a spaceship.

Arthropods
Eight-legged creatures have been launched into orbit, including golden orb spiders and South African flat rock scorpions.

Cats
Felix was the first cat in space. Launched on a French rocket on October 18, 1963, the flying feline survived the mission.

WHICH WAY IS UP?

SOME ANIMALS seem to have very little trouble adapting in outer Space. Mice for instance, groom themselves as they float in their cages, seemingly unfazed by the lack of gravity. But tadpoles and fish swim in loops rather than in straight lines, say NASA scientists, because they can't figure out which way is up and which is down.

Chimpanzees

Americans launched the first chimp into space on January 31, 1963. "Astrochimp" Ham was sent on a suborbital flight aboard a Mercury rocket and came home safely.

Dogs

The Soviet Union was the first country to send dogs into space. Pooches Tsygan and Dezik were launched into suborbital flight on January 29, 1951, and both dogs survived the mission.

Fish and Other Underwater Creatures

Fish and sea creatures of all sorts have accompanied astronauts in space labs. Brine shrimp, carp, Japanese killifish, medaka, mumichog, oyster toadfish, sea urchins, swordtail fish, tardigrades, and zebra danio are among the many species sent into space.

Insects

Scores of insect species have been sent into orbit: carpenter bees, crickets, desert beetles, flour beetles, fruit flies (the very first living things ever launched into space, by the United States in 1947), harvester ants, meal worms, Madagascar hissing cockroaches, parasitic wasps, seed-harvester ants, silkworms, and wine flies.

Monkeys

Monkeys were some of the first space voyagers, including, macaques, rhesus monkeys, and squirrel monkeys.

Rodents

Guinea pigs, mice, and rats have all made the trip into space.

Other Species of Space Travelers

Nematodes, snails, and even tortoises have gone to space!

One of the world's first "cosmonauts," Russian space dog Belka poses after a successful mission aboard *Sputnik 5*.

AN ORBITING ZOO

On April 17, 1998, NASA launched into space more than 2,000 animals—18 pregnant mice, 135 snails, 152 rats, 233 fish, and 1,514 crickets—for an important 16-day mission. This motley crew (along with one woman and six men) boarded the Space Shuttle *Columbia* as part of the NEUROLAB project. NEUROLAB's goal was to study how being in space affects the brain and behavior. Their findings are helping scientists understand more about motion sickness, insomnia, dizziness, and other challenges faced by astronauts—and those of us who never leave Earth.

That's one weird fish! An oyster toadfish (*Opsanus tau*), like those that are part of the NEUROLAB mission aboard the Space Shuttle *Columbia*, takes a swim in its holding tank in the Space Station Processing Facility.

Just one week after its creation, on October 7, 1958, NASA unveiled Project Mercury. Its goals: to send a human into space to orbit Earth and to bring him and his spacecraft back home safely, and to learn how spaceflight affects the human body. NASA's next task was to choose the men who would make this pioneering journey into space.

You Must Be This Short to Ride

As NASA sought applicants for the first flights into space, it focused on experience and education: applicants had to be military jet pilots who had graduated from test pilot school and had 1,500 hours of flying time. They also were required to be less than 40 years old and have a bachelor's degree in engineering. But there was also a physical requirement: no one taller than 5-feet, 11 inches could apply to be an astronaut. Why? Anyone taller than

that could not fit into the capsule. More than 500 men were eligible for the job, but only seven would be chosen.

Ill-Fated Russian Flights

Around the time the names of the Mercury astronauts were being announced, the Soviets had already launched—and lost—three cosmonauts.

The men died in separate flights in 1957, 1958, and 1959. Their missions were not designed to leave Earth's orbit but rather to reach the outer atmosphere and then return to Earth. The existence of those missions, and those cosmonauts' names (Ledovskikh, Shaborin, and Mitkov) were not released until 2001. Those deaths led the Russians to take cosmonaut training more seriously. That in turn may have contributed to the Soviets putting the first man in space, Yuri Gagarin (1934–1968), on April 12, 1961.

This interesting contraption, known as a Gimbal Rig, was used to train astronauts how to keep their composure and maintain control of their spacecraft in the event that it went into a spin.

TESTING . . . TESTING . . .

ASTRO APPLICANTS WERE subjected to rigorous tests of their physical and psychological abilities. Some of the more "interesting" ways that NASA gauged a pilot's readiness to venture into space included plunging his feet into a bucket of ice water and measuring his heart rate and pulse before and after; placing him in a room heated to 130°F for two hours; and locking him in a dark, soundproof room for three hours to monitor his ability to adapt to unusual circumstances and a lack of interaction with anyone, or anything, else.

Astronaut John Glenn undergoes training in a space capsule simulator.

AND THE WINNERS ARE . . .

ON APRIL 9, 1959, in a NASA press conference, America was introduced to the seven Mercury astronauts. They were:

1. **Scott Carpenter** (b. 1925), navy pilot
2. **L. Gordon Cooper** (1927–2004), air force pilot
3. **John H. Glenn Jr.** (b. 1921), Marine Corps pilot
4. **Virgil I. "Gus" Grissom** (1926–1967), air force pilot
5. **Walter M. Schirra Jr.** (1923–2007), navy pilot
6. **Alan B. Shepard Jr.** (1923–1998), navy pilot
7. **Donald K. "Deke" Slayton** (1924–1993), air force pilot

The Mercury Seven: Back row (left to right) Alan Shepard, Gus Grissom, Gordon Cooper. Front row (left to right) Wally Schirra, Deke Slayton, John Glenn, and Scott Carpenter

As American newspapers trumpeted his accomplishment, Russian cosmonaut Yuri Gagarin became a highly decorated hero back in the Soviet Union.

The Huntsville Times

Feature Index

	Page		Page
Abby	14	Editorials	4
Amusements	6	Sports	22
Comics	25	Society	5
Crossword	28	Want Ads	26
Jumble	14	Radio-TV	26

28 PAGES TODAY

VOL. 51, NO. 21   CHICAGO DAILY NEWS SERVICE   HUNTSVILLE, ALABAMA, WEDNESDAY, APR. 12, 1961   ASSOCIATED PRESS — WIREPHOTO   45c PER WEEK

Where Progress...

Covers The Valley!

Man Enters Space

'So Close, Yet So Far,' Sighs Cape

U.S. Had Hoped For Own Launch

CANAVERAL, Fla. (AP) — The Redstone the United States had hoped would boost ...to space stands on a launching pad ...Union beat its firing date by at least ...

"...so far," commented a technician who ...the Redstone to send one of America's astronauts on a short sub-orbital flight, hopefully late this month or early in May.

"If we hadn't had those troubles last fall and on the chimp and Little Joe shots this year, we might have made it," the technician said.

"But you have to give the Russian scientists credit. They've accomplished a remarkable breakthrough."

Dr. Hugh Dryden, deputy direc...

Soviet Officer Orbits Globe In 5-Ton Ship

Maximum Height Reached Reported As 188 Miles

MOSCOW (AP)—A Soviet astronaut has orbited the globe for more than a... hour and returned safely to receive the plaudits of scientists and political leaders alike. Soviet announcement of the feat brought praise from President Kennedy and U. S. space experts left behind in the contest to put the first man into suc... cessful space flight.

By the Soviet account, Maj. Yuri Alekseyvich Gargarin, rode a five-to... spaceship once around the earth in an orbit taking an hour and 20 minutes. H... was in the air a total of an hour and 48 minutes.

The whole sequence of events and the announcements relating to it raised a number of questions. The Soviet announcement said the flight took place today between 9:07 and 10:55 a.m., but some persons in Moscow's Western colony were skeptical about the...

VON BRAUN'S REACTION:

'To Keep Up, U.S...

Must Run L...

The Mercury Missions

Project Mercury (1959–1963) was one of history's firsts: it sent the first American into space (in a suborbital flight) and the first into orbit around Earth. With its total of 20 unmanned and six manned flights, Project Mercury launched America into the space race.

Shepard Leads the Way

At dawn on May 5, 1961, astronaut Alan Shepard climbed into *Freedom 7*, the Mercury capsule that would make him the first American in space. The pressure was on: three weeks earlier, the Soviet Union's Yuri Gagarin became the first human being in space and the first human to orbit Earth. America needed a successful flight.

After waiting on the launch pad for almost four hours, Shepard and *Freedom 7* finally lifted off toward space and into the history books. The suborbital flight took a little under 16 minutes as *Freedom 7* flew to an altitude of 116 miles and reached a peak velocity of 5,134 miles per hour.

Prior to becoming an astronaut, Alan Shepard was an accomplished navy pilot.

After a long wait on the launch pad, *Freedom 7* finally blasts off carrying the first American into space.

Alan Shepard sits in the Mercury capsule for a flight simulation test one week before his actual mission.

Lucky Number Seven

Although the Soviets downplayed Shepard's flight as being a lesser accomplishment than Gagarin's, it nevertheless set the stage for five more successful Mercury missions. In fact, the only astronaut of the original seven who did not make a trip into space during Project Mercury was Deke Slayton, who was unable to fly due to a heart condition. More than a decade later, however, he received medical clearance and finally made it into space.

MERCURY MILESTONES

Freedom 7, May 5, 1961: Alan Shepard becomes the first American in space.

Liberty Bell 7, July 21, 1961: Gus Grissom flies the second 15-minute suborbital flight. Shortly after splashdown, the spacecraft sinks, but Grissom is unhurt.

Friendship 7, February 20, 1962: John Glenn becomes the first American to orbit Earth. His three-orbit flight lasts 4 hours, 55 minutes, 23 seconds.

Aurora 7, May 24, 1962: Scott Carpenter confirms John Glenn's success with a second three-orbit flight.

Sigma 7, October 3, 1962: Astronaut Wally Schirra orbits Earth six times.

Faith 7, May 15–16 1963: During this the final Mercury mission, Gordon Cooper orbits Earth 22 times in 34 hours, 19 minutes, 49 seconds.

Above, John Glenn carefully slips into the cramped confines of the *Freedom 7* capsule.

DID YOU KNOW?

The Mercury capsule was only 11½ feet high and just over 6 feet in diameter. Filled with switches and controls, astronauts were said to "wear" it rather than sit in it.

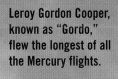

Leroy Gordon Cooper, known as "Gordo," flew the longest of all the Mercury flights.

The Gemini Missions

With the Gemini program, NASA wanted to test its equipment and prepare its astronauts for longer space journeys—up to two weeks in length. Two astronauts would fly on each of the 10 human Gemini missions (named appropriately, after the astrological sign, Gemini, the Twins), which readied humans and machines for a trip to the moon.

Project Gemini was an ambitious undertaking in that all 10 of these flights would take place within a short two-year window. It began with *Gemini 3* in March 1965—which tested the spaceship's maneuverability while in orbit—and concluded with *Gemini 12* in November 1966. In between, this program saw several "firsts," including the first U.S. spacewalk.

Stepping Outside

The first spacewalk by an American took place on June 3, 1965. Astronaut Ed White (1930–1967) had the honor as he floated out of the *Gemini 4* capsule for a 23-minute EVA (extra-vehicular activity, as spacewalks are known at NASA). White propelled himself to and from the capsule three times on the 26-foot tether. He enjoyed his walk so much that his crewmate, James McDivitt (b. 1929), had to beg him to return to the craft.

But after the spacewalk, McDivitt and White were unable to close the craft's door tightly and were forced to make a repair using previously untested tools. The repair was successful and the capsule safely returned to Earth.

Astronaut Ed White takes a walk outside his *Gemini 4* capsule. In his right hand is a control unit that helps to move him around in zero-gravity space.

WALK ON THE WILD SIDE

PRIOR TO AMERICA accomplishing the feat, the first human to walk in space was Soviet cosmonaut Alexei Leonov (b. 1934), who embarked from his *Voskhod 2* spacecraft on March 18, 1965, for what would be a 10-minute experiment. But the adventure nearly cost Leonov his life: his spacesuit malfunctioned, blowing up like a balloon and tightening around him. He had trouble getting into the airlock, the chamber between the outside of the craft and the oxygenated safety of *Voskhod 2*. After struggling for several minutes—during which time he perspired so much that sweat filled the suit nearly to his ankles—he finally reached the safety of the craft.

Part of *Gemini 9*'s mission was an attempt to link up with this docking target. The target's protective cover never fully opened, which led the crew to refer to it as an "angry alligator."

TAKEOUT FOOD

DURING THE EARLY days of human space flight, the food available to astronauts was not exactly tasty. Project Mercury crews sucked applesauce out of heavy metal tubes or ate dry, pressed cubes of raisins, cereal, and nuts, all coated in gelatin.

Gus Grissom complained so much about the freeze-dried menu that his fellow astronauts decided to treat him to something different during his March 1965 *Gemini 3* flight. Wally Schirra passed a corned beef sandwich (Grissom's favorite) to John W. Young (b. 1930), who would be flying with Grissom on the five-hour mission. When the craft reached its orbit, Young surprised Grissom with the sandwich. But as Grissom began to eat, bits of beef and crumbs from the rye bread began to float around the cabin. Luckily, none of it lodged in or damaged equipment.

Back on Earth, NASA was not amused. And once the prank was made public, neither was Congress, which extracted a promise from NASA's deputy administrator that there would be no "recurrence of corned beef sandwiches on future flights."

John Young (left) and Gus Grissom (right), the first astronauts to bring a corned beef sandwich into space.

Early Apollo Missions

On May 25, 1961—just a few weeks after Alan Shepard became the first American in space—President John F. Kennedy addressed a joint session of Congress about the economy, foreign relations, and other issues. Toward the end of this speech, Kennedy turned to the issue of space exploration. "I believe," he said, "that this nation should commit itself to achieving the goal, before this decade is out, of landing a man on the moon and returning him safely to the earth."

Project Apollo (1963–1972) was the program that would fulfill the president's lunar landing objective. But before the historic moonwalk of *Apollo 11* could take place, much preparation was required to get both human and machine ready for this ambitious undertaking.

Unmanned Tests

The Apollo spacecraft itself was composed of three sections: the command module, where the crew would spend most of its time; the service module, which was

EARTHRISE

It was during the *Apollo 8* flight that astronaut William Anders snapped one of the world's most famous photographs. During the craft's third orbit of the moon, the crew was busily taking pictures of its surface. At one point, Commander Frank Borman caught sight of the earth rising over the gray and craggy surface of the moon. Astronaut Anders—who had a color camera—took the photograph, which came to be known as "Earthrise." It became one of the most recognized and published photographs in history.

basically the power plant of the ship; and the lunar module, which would land on the moon and return back to the ship. Early uncrewed missions tested each of these modules as well as other systems on the spacecraft. *Apollo 6* would be the final unmanned test flight.

A Crew of Three

Launched on October 11, 1968, *Apollo 7* was the first human mission in the program. Each of the Apollo flights would carry three astronauts into space. Of those early human flights, two (*Apollo 7* and *9*) orbited the earth and two (*Apollo 8* and *10*) orbited the moon.

DID YOU KNOW?

There were no flights called *Apollo 2* or *Apollo 3*. That's because the designation "Apollo" wasn't officially chosen as the program's name until the fourth mission. What came to be known as *Apollo 1* had originally been designated Apollo 204, because the space vehicle was the AS-204.

The *Apollo 7* crew in their spacesuits (left to right): Wally Schirra, Donn Eisele (1930–1987), and Walter Cunningham (b. 1932)

THE SATURN V ROCKET

THE LARGEST ROCKET ever launched—the Saturn V —rose to a height of 363 feet, taller than a 36-story building, and weighed 6 million pounds. It was also the world's most powerful rocket, containing as much energy as an atomic bomb. And every bit of that energy would be required for Apollo's lofty goals.

First launched during the unmanned *Apollo 4* mission, the rocket was a resounding success. It performed equally well during its second human flight, the historic *Apollo 8* mission. During that flight, which launched on December 21, 1968, and returned to Earth on December 27, 1968, astronauts Frank Borman (b. 1928), James A. Lovell (b. 1928), and William A. Anders (b. 1933) orbited the moon 10 times.

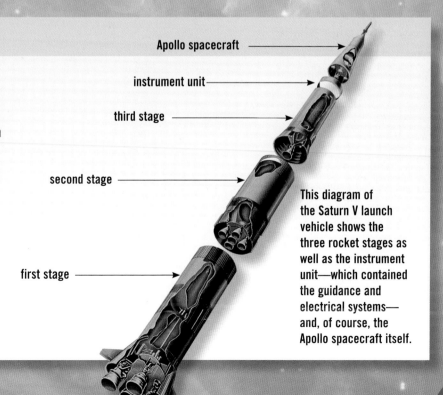

Apollo spacecraft

instrument unit

third stage

second stage

first stage

This diagram of the Saturn V launch vehicle shows the three rocket stages as well as the instrument unit—which contained the guidance and electrical systems— and, of course, the Apollo spacecraft itself.

Landing on the Moon

It was 9:32 AM on July 16, 1969, that astronauts Neil Armstrong (b. 1930), Edward "Buzz" Aldrin (b. 1930), and Michael Collins (b. 1930) embarked on an historic 236,121-mile journey to the moon, fulfilling a goal set by President John F. Kennedy six years before. On July 20, the third day of the flight, the *Eagle* lunar landing craft separated from the *Columbia* command module and descended from its orbit 70 miles above the moon's surface.

But there was a problem: the previously chosen landing site turned out to be strewn with boulders. And so, with just 114 seconds of fuel remaining, the crew manually landed the *Eagle* in an area called the Sea of Tranquility. The crew was too excited to take the four-hour nap that had been scheduled for them. Instead, they readied the *Eagle* for a speedy departure, in case it was necessary, and then Neil Armstrong left the lunar lander, carefully backed down its steps, and became the first person to set foot on the moon.

Left Behind

When the astronauts of *Apollo 11* returned safely to Earth, they brought with them 60 pounds of moon rocks and

MAKE THAT "A" MAN

AS NEIL ARMSTRONG stepped onto the surface of the moon at 10:56:15 PM EDT on July 20, 1969, he uttered the phrase: "That's one small step for man, one giant leap for mankind." What he had *meant* to say was, "That's one small step for *a* man, one giant leap for mankind." But in his excitement, Armstrong goofed up the line. And who could blame him? He was about to be the very first human being to touch the moon. Who wouldn't have butterflies?

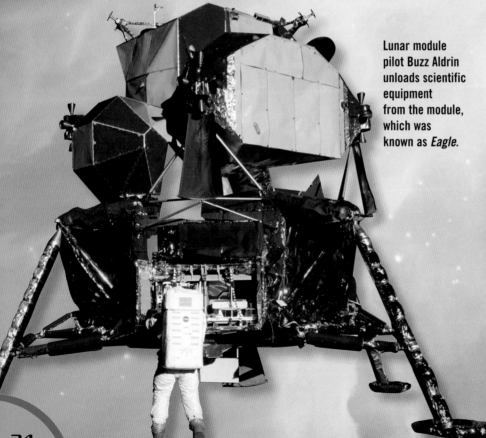

Lunar module pilot Buzz Aldrin unloads scientific equipment from the module, which was known as *Eagle*.

The *Apollo 11* crew (left to right): Neil Armstrong, Michael Collins, and Buzz Aldrin

some soil samples. But the astronauts left behind several items, too, among them an American flag; a disk with recorded statements by presidents Eisenhower, Kennedy, Johnson, and Nixon and 73 other world leaders; some scientific instruments; and a plaque that reads "Here men from the planet Earth first set foot upon the moon. July 1969 AD We came in peace for all mankind."

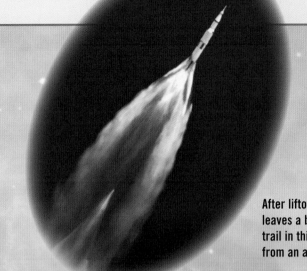

After liftoff, *Apollo 11* leaves a brilliant fiery trail in this photo taken from an air force plane.

DID YOU KNOW?

Was the moon-landing faked—a stunt acted out on a Hollywood set to distract Americans from the Vietnam War or increase the United States's prestige during the Cold War? That's what some conspiracy theorists believe. Of course, the *Apollo 11* did, in fact, land on the moon—as did five other Apollo missions.

This famous photo of Buzz Aldrin was taken by fellow astronaut Neil Armstrong, whose reflection can be seen in Aldrin's visor.

Launched on Saturday, April 11, 1970, *Apollo 13* was to be the third U.S. mission to land on the moon. Crewmembers Jim Lovell (b. 1928), John Swigert (1931–1982), and Fred Haise (b. 1933) had no inkling that the mission would be anything but successful.

200,000 Miles from Home

But two days into the flight, disaster struck: a malfunction caused one of the craft's two oxygen tanks to explode and the other to fail, damaging the service module in the process. Then, two of three fuel cells failed. Not only were the command and service modules without power and water, but

the astronauts were also rapidly running out of oxygen. The command module (CM) had a back-up battery, but that needed to be reserved for the return to Earth.

Landing on the moon was out of the question. With the astronauts 200,000 miles from home and oxygen running out quickly, the focus now was on getting the astronauts safely back to Earth.

What Now?

A plan was devised: because oxygen was running out in the CM, the three men would move into the lunar module (LM) for the return to Earth. Once they were within a few hours of splashdown, they would move back into the CM.

The LM was designed to keep two astronauts alive for two days; the three-man *Apollo 13* crew would have to live in it for four days. The men huddled in

DID YOU KNOW?

The story of the *Apollo 13* flight was so dramatic that it was made into a 1995 movie, *Apollo 13,* directed by Ron Howard and starring Tom Hanks. The film's screenplay was adapted from a book co-authored by mission commander Jim Lovell.

NASA's mission control room erupts with applause, thumbs up signals, and celebratory cigars after the safe return of the *Apollo 13* astronauts.

the tiny LM, and for four days carefully rationed their water and power.

Once *Apollo 13* was nearing reentry, the crew—near freezing and dehydrated—returned to the CM. But their ordeal was not over. Without enough power to navigate by computer, the crew would have to align the CM manually to reenter Earth's atmosphere.

Amazingly, the plan worked, and nearly a week after it began, the mission of *Apollo 13* came to a safe end as the CM splashed down in the Pacific.

UNLUCKY 13

THE NUMBER "13" crops up quite a lot with regard to *Apollo 13*. Was that famously unlucky number responsible for the flight's mishaps? You be the judge!

- The flight was launched on April 11, 1970, or 4/11/70—4 + 1 + 1 + 7 = 13.

- Launch time was 1:13 PM Houston time— or 13:13 in military time.

- The mishap that caused the oxygen tank to explode occurred on April 13 (although it was a Monday, not a Friday).

Crew aboard the USS *Iwo Jima* lift the *Apollo 13* command module out of the Pacific Ocean.

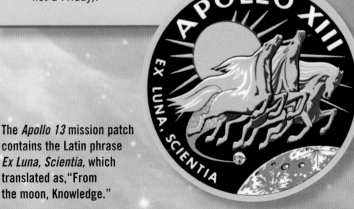

The *Apollo 13* mission patch contains the Latin phrase *Ex Luna, Scientia,* which translated as, "From the moon, Knowledge."

The lucky crew of Apollo 13 (left to right) Fred Haise, John Swigert, and James Lovell returned to a rousing welcome aboard the USS *Iwo Jima.*

Apollo 15

The fourth Apollo mission to land a human on the moon was a mission of firsts. Launched on July 26, 1971, *Apollo 15*'s crewmembers—David Scott (b. 1932), James Irwin (1930–1991), and Alfred Worden (b. 1932)—had with them the Lunar Roving Vehicle, or lunar rover, which made its debut on their mission. This lunar "dune buggy" allowed the astronauts to extend the range of their explorations of the moon—to 17 miles on *Apollo 15*, compared to just two miles on *Apollo 14*.

More Time on the Moon

Apollo 15 was also the first of three missions during which astronauts would spend longer periods of time exploring the moon itself. For instance, *Apollo 14*'s crew spent a total of 9 hours on the lunar surface, while the *Apollo 15* crew explored for nearly 19 hours over the course of three days.

In addition to allowing astronauts to travel farther and faster, the Lunar Roving Vehicle allowed them to carry more rock samples back to the Lunar Lander. On the moon, the rover could carry 1,080 pounds of rocks and other material (on Earth, the same amount would weigh nearly 6,500 pounds).

DID YOU KNOW?

The Saturn V rocket that propelled *Apollo 15*—and all of the other Apollo missions—traveled at a rate of six miles per second—which is around *13 times faster* than a bullet fired from a rifle. That kind of power is necessary for a spacecraft to escape Earth's gravitational pull.

From left, David Scott, Alfred Worden, and James Irwin, crew of *Apollo 15*. Only Scott and Irwin landed on the moon, while Worden stayed in the command module. He can claim the distinction of "most isolated human being," because while his crewmates were on the moon he was farther away from other humans—2,235 miles—than anyone else has ever been.

Ancient Rock

One of *Apollo 15*'s most notable accomplishments was the discovery of what the press dubbed the "Genesis Rock." After extensive testing, scientists back on Earth determined that the grapefruit-sized rock may have been part of the moon's original crust and was at least 4.15 billion years old. Analysis of that rock helped scientists learn more about how the moon was created—and about the age of the entire solar system.

The Genesis Rock dates to the earliest days of our solar system, when the sun was young and the planets were forming. Scott and Irwin picked up this rock on the second of three EVAs.

GALILEO WAS RIGHT!

BACK IN THE seventeenth century, Italian astronomer, mathematician, philosopher, and physicist Galileo Galilei theorized that gravity acts on all objects equally. In other words, if you were to drop a 10-pound weight and a 1-pound weight from a tower in a vacuum at the same time, they would land at the same time. This was pretty revolutionary, because for a thousand years before that, people believed that the heavier object would fall faster and land first.

Fast-forward to 1971 and the end of the final *Apollo 15* moonwalk. Turning to a camera that had been set up earlier, astronaut David Scott spoke:

In my left hand I have a feather, in my right hand, a hammer. And I guess one of the reasons we got here today was because of a gentleman named Galileo, a long time ago, who made a rather significant discovery about falling objects in gravity fields. And we thought, "Where would be a better place to confirm his findings than on the moon?" And so we thought we'd try it here for you . . . I'll drop the two of them here and hopefully they'll hit the ground at the same time.

Scott let go of the feather and the hammer at the same time and . . . both hit the lunar surface at the same time, leading Scott to report, "How about that! Mr. Galileo was correct in his findings!"

David Scott, mission commander, salutes an American flag on the moon. The lunar module is behind him; James Irwin is behind the camera. The astronauts' footprints are clearly visible in the lunar dust.

The Apollo Legacy

Between 1963 and 1972, the Apollo missions put 12 Americans on the moon and returned them home safely, achieving President Kennedy's original goal for the program. But increased scientific understanding of the moon is not all that we gained from those years of exploration. The Apollo program also gave us knowledge and technology that has made everyday life better here on Earth.

Clean Water and Safe Fabrics

Because space and power were limited in the Apollo spacecrafts, NASA needed a water purification system that wouldn't use too much energy or take up too much space. It worked with a private company to come up with one that was just a little bigger than a deck of cards. Today, that technology is used to purify water in households and communities all around the world.

After the three *Apollo 1* astronauts died when their capsule caught fire, NASA worked to develop fire-resistant fabrics for space suits and vehicles. Those same materials are now used to protect firefighters and soldiers, among others.

The astronauts' space suits benefited other items, too: many of today's cushioned athletic shoes, cooling fabrics worn by race car drivers, even an environmentally friendly Teflon-coated fiberglass roofing material, were all based on the very same space suits designed to keep the Apollo astronauts safe and comfortable.

The water-purification system developed by NASA for the Apollo program was the predecessor for the jug-and-filter system that may be in your home's refrigerator right now.

LEFT BEHIND

TWELVE APOLLO ASTRONAUTS landed on the moon—and they didn't arrive empty-handed. In fact, Americans left behind more than 100 items on the lunar surface. Here are just a few.

- American flag
- Bottom portion of the lunar lander
- Containers for urine and feces
- One pair of Neil Armstrong's space boots
- Several cameras, their various lenses, and a tripod
- Three lunar rovers (at $38 million apiece!)
- Two (empty) food bags
- Two golf balls, both hit by Alan Shepard
- Various tools used to dig and collect rock and dust samples

But, Americans weren't the only lunar litterbugs. India, Japan, and the old USSR all have landed (or crash-landed) crewless spacecraft on the moon. Perhaps the next time astronauts land on the moon, they'll remember the old adage: *Take only photographs, leave only footprints.*

Hadley Rille
15

Taurus-Littrow
17

Sea of Tranquility
11

Ocean of Storms | Fra Mauro
12   14

Descartes
16

Apollo Lunar Landing Mission Locations

11	*Apollo 11.* Landed July 20, 1969
12	*Apollo 12.* Landed November 19, 1969
14	*Apollo 14.* Landed February 5, 1971
15	*Apollo 15.* Landed July 30, 1971
16	*Apollp 16.* Landed April 20, 1972
17	*Apollo 17.* Landed December 11, 1972

Because the moon's rotation (on its axis) is perfectly in sync with its orbit (around the earth), the six Apollo landing sites always face Earth. The sites were chosen because they were geologically varied and would give the astronauts a chance to collect different types of soil and rock.

MOON TREES?

When the crew of *Apollo 14* blasted off for the moon, they had with them hundreds of tree seeds from the National Forest Service. Those seeds orbited the moon with astronaut Stuart Roosa (1933–1994) in the command module while his crewmates explored the lunar surface. Once back on Earth, the seeds (from Douglas fir, loblolly pine, redwood, sweetgum, and sycamore trees) were planted around the country—one ended up at the White House—and they're still growing and healthy today.

Approximately 450 seeds traveled to and from space with *Apollo 14*. Almost all of the trees sprouted. This one, a sycamore, was planted in Philadelphia's Washington Square on May 6, 1975.

Working in Space

In the year 1900, at the beginning of the twentieth century, humans could not fly, let alone travel beyond Earth's atmosphere. But barely 70 years later, humans had not only journeyed to the moon, but they had walked upon its surface as well. What would come next?

Once the goal of reaching the moon had been achieved and the Apollo program concluded in 1972, NASA turned its attention to putting astronauts into space for longer periods, during which they could conduct experiments. Space stations were the orbiting laboratories in which these men and women would live and work.

The Soviet Union sent the world's first space station into space, in 1971. In fact, the Soviets would launch three space stations before NASA launched its first.

Salyut 1 and Skylab

The Soviet Union launched the unmanned *Salyut 1* space station on April 19, 1971. The only cosmonauts to board the station were the crew of *Soyuz 11*. For 23 days, Georgi Dobrovolski, Vladislav, and Viktor Patsayev conducted experiments and performed maintenance on the station before returning to Earth. Sadly, their capsule depressurized during the descent, and the crew suffocated. *Salyut 1* reentered Earth's atmosphere on October 11, 1971.

Skylab, the first U.S. space station, was launched unmanned on May 14, 1973. For six years, the station stayed in orbit. Three crews visited the station—the longest stay was 84 days. While there, the crews performed nearly 300 experiments and gathered information about subjects ranging from the effects of prolonged weightlessness on humans to the behavior of the Comet Kohoutek.

The Sky(lab) is Falling!

After the last crew left *Skylab* in early February 1974, it remained in low orbit for several more years. NASA had planned to send a shuttle crew to the station sometime in the 1980s, but before that could happen,

Skylab flies high above the earth in an image taken by *Skylab 4* crewmembers, the last to visit the station.

solar activity severely disturbed the station's orbit and sent it careening toward Earth. Tracking the falling space station's descent became a national pastime; radio stations and newspapers offered rewards to listeners who produced a piece of the doomed craft.

In the end, *Skylab* fell to Earth in mid-July 1979, its debris scattered in the Indian Ocean and Western Australia. One town in which debris fell issued a $400 littering fine to the United States.

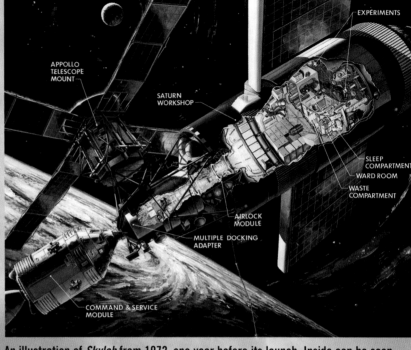

An illustration of *Skylab* from 1972, one year before its launch. Inside can be seen the crew's sleeping and living quarters. Each *Skylab* mission sent three astronauts to the station.

Gerald Carr, *Skylab 4* commander, pretends to lift crewmember William Pogue upside-down on one finger. The pair was goofing off in the zero-gravity weightlessness of space.

DID YOU KNOW?

Long stays in space can be very difficult, physically and mentally. Long workdays can make the problems worse. The crew of *Skylab 4* were so overworked and overstressed that the three men staged what's become known as the "24-hour mutiny," during which they simply rested. Today, rest days and plenty of exercise are part of any stay at the space station.

An artist's conception of the Apollo-Soyuz Test Project, which connected the American Apollo spacecraft to the Soviet Union's *Soyuz*. The project, launched in 1975, was an important step in developing international cooperation in space.

Space Station Partners

The International Space Station as it appeared in 2001, from the Space Shuttle *Discovery*

Look into the night sky on the right evening, and you'll see it: the International Space Station (ISS), a state-of-the-art research laboratory that orbits Earth at approximately 240 miles above its surface. In this 15,000-square-foot facility, crews of astronauts from all over the world live and work, carrying out medical experiments and testing communications and industrial equipment and tools. Construction on the space station began in 1998, when the first module—the Russian-built *Zarya*—was launched. Since then, the space station has grown larger as modules built by different countries are added. Canada, for instance, contributed a robotic arm that functions as a crane; Japan constructed a lab for the space station; and the United States built an airlock, which functions as a doorway from the station to space.

Crews usually stay aboard the ISS for six months at a time, although one Russian cosmonaut stayed there for 2.2 years. The zero-gravity environment of the space stations allows astronauts to perform experiments that are not possible on Earth. For instance, it's been discovered that some germs become more infectious after being exposed to a micro-gravity environment. Knowing that can help scientists find ways to make them less infectious.

Astronauts frequently conduct Education Downlinks. These 20-minute question-and-answer sessions allow students and teachers to talk with crewmembers using just a television and a phone line.

THE WHO'S WHO OF THE INTERNATIONAL SPACE STATION

ONCE THE INTERNATIONAL Space Station is complete, it will have benefited from the contributions of 16 countries.

- Belgium
- Brazil
- Canada
- Denmark
- France
- Germany

- Italy
- Japan
- Netherlands
- Norway
- Russia
- Spain

- Sweden
- Switzerland
- United Kingdom
- United States

Zarya (Russian for "dawn") is 41 feet long and 13 feet wide at its thickest point. Its two solar arrays, which splay out to either side of the module, are each 35 by 11 feet, and allow the station to generate power from the sun.

Astronaut Stephen Robinson, of Space Shuttle *Discovery* mission STS-114, works high above Earth while tethered to Canadarm2, a 56-foot-long robotic arm attached to the International Space Station.

LIVING IN SPACE

HEADING TO SPACE sounds like an exciting adventure, but life aboard the space station poses some challenges, too. Here are just a few.

- **Motion sickness.** About half of all astronauts suffer from nausea and stomach upset. They take drugs to combat the symptoms.

- **Stuffy head.** Living in an environment with very little gravity causes the fluids in the body to rise to the head. That can make an astronaut feel like he or she has a head cold all of the time.

- **Toilet trials**. Going to the bathroom in zero gravity means strapping oneself onto the toilet and "going" into a tube. The whole thing works a little like a vacuum cleaner.

DID YOU KNOW?

The research and experiments that astronaut/ scientists are performing in space will have wide-ranging effects in space and on Earth. The crew of the International Space Station routinely photographs the earth, providing us with a record of how we change and impact the planet. The growth of cities, expansion of farmland, and even changes caused by floods and volcanic eruptions are all noted.

An image of Hurricane Ivan in the Caribbean Sea, taken by International Space Station astronaut Edward M. Fincke. Tracking storms like Ivan from space allows people back on Earth to better predict their strength and likely path.

Space Shuttles

NASA sometimes refers to the space shuttles as its fleet of "workhorses." That's because over the course of the shuttle program's nearly 30-year, 130-mission duration, shuttles and their crews have performed the day-in and day-out tasks that keep the United States in space. They have launched, retrieved, rescued, and repaired satellites; tested tools and equipment; and delivered crews, supplies, and parts to the International Space Station.

DID YOU KNOW?

The space shuttle orbiter travels roughly 4.5 million miles on each flight. But the wheels on each shuttle are replaced after just one landing!

In order to save weight and therefore fuel, NASA stripped down the two 747s that transport the oribiter to Florida. The added weight causes the plane to use more than twice as much fuel as it would flying without the shuttle orbiter.

IT'S *NOT* AN AIRPLANE

THE SPACE SHUTTLE is not an airplane—it's more like a glider. Because it has no engines to help it climb, the shuttle has only one chance to land. No engines also means that if the shuttle lands in California, it must be "carried" back to Florida, where it is launched. When that happens, the shuttle is attached to the top of a specially outfitted 747 airplane and "piggybacked" back home.

Lots of Mileage

One of the most technologically advanced features of the space shuttles is that they—along with their solid rocket boosters—are the first reusable crafts. In fact, at last count, the Space Shuttle *Discovery* has flown 38 missions, each one covering roughly 4.5 million miles. The solid rocket boosters are used approximately 25 times before they are replaced.

The Space Shuttle *Atlantis* lifts off on a mission to the International Space Station. *Atlantis* was named for a sailing ship that explored the oceans from the 1930s to the 1960s.

Anatomy of a Shuttle

If you look at a picture of the shuttle on its launchpad, you can easily see its parts. What you probably think of as being the actual "shuttle" is also called the orbiter. That's where the crew (usually three to seven people) lives and works for the duration of the mission.

To either side of the shuttle orbiter are the two solid rocket boosters. These important rockets—the most powerful in the world—propel the shuttle off of the launchpad during the first two minutes of flight. Once the shuttle escapes Earth's gravitational pull, the boosters separate from the shuttle. It is then that parachutes open and the boosters gently fall into the ocean, where carriers retrieve them.

The large orange structure is called the external tank (ET). That's a liquid-fuel tank; its job is to propel the shuttle into orbit, an altitude of about 71 miles. Once there (and after about 8½ minutes) the ET is jettisoned. It comes apart and then falls into the ocean.

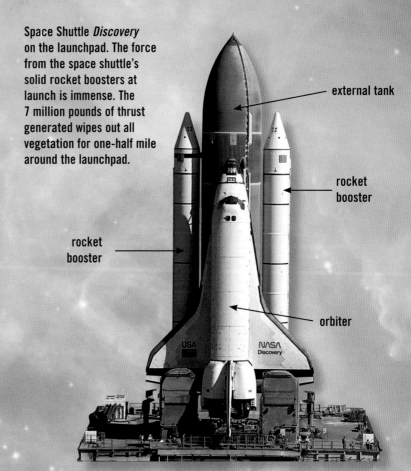

Space Shuttle *Discovery* on the launchpad. The force from the space shuttle's solid rocket boosters at launch is immense. The 7 million pounds of thrust generated wipes out all vegetation for one-half mile around the launchpad.

external tank

rocket booster

rocket booster

orbiter

Parts of the space shuttle. As the first reusable spacecraft, the shuttle orbiter is complex and very durable. And yet, it cannot land in the rain. Why? The tiles on its underside—although they can withstand 2,500-degree temperatures—are so delicate that rain would destroy them.

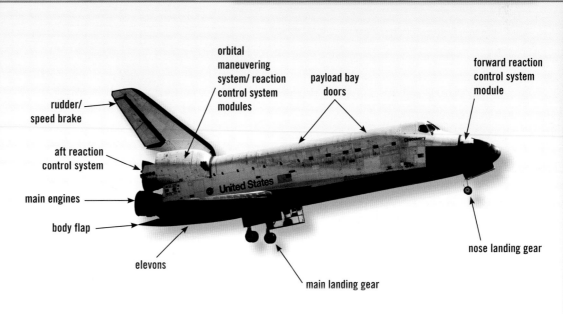

orbital maneuvering system/ reaction control system modules

payload bay doors

forward reaction control system module

rudder/ speed brake

aft reaction control system

main engines

body flap

elevons

main landing gear

nose landing gear

Shuttle Firsts

Because the shuttle program has been in existence for so long and began when space exploration was still in its relative infancy, it can boast several "firsts." Dr. Sally Ride, physicist, author, and educator, became the first American woman in space when she flew as a crewmember on the Space Shuttle *Challenger* in 1983; it was the seventh shuttle mission.

Space Guy

The space shuttle program also put the first African-American into space. Air force pilot Guion "Guy" Bluford flew as a mission specialist on the Space Shuttle *Challenger* during the program's eighth flight in 1983. That year also marked the first time six crewmembers had ever flown together in a single spacecraft.

Guy Bluford flew on four shuttle missions between 1983 and 1992. Dr. Bluford spent a total of 688 hours in space working on the space station and testing flight software.

Sally Ride was a mission specialist on two shuttle missions. She also served on the committee that investigated the Space Shuttle *Challenger* disaster. In 2001, Dr. Ride founded Sally Ride Science, a company that helps kids learn about science, math, and technology.

WHO'S WHO ON A SHUTTLE FLIGHT

THERE ARE THREE different kinds of astronauts on each space shuttle flight:

- **The Commander** is the person in charge. He or she is responsible for the success of the mission and the safety of the crew.

- **The Pilot** helps the commander to operate the shuttle. He or she also manages the details of the mission projects, such as repairing satellites.

- **Each Mission Specialist**—and there can be several on each mission—has one area of responsibility. Maybe that's performing a medical experiment or testing a piece of equipment.

No Strings Attached!

The first untethered spacewalk—one in which the astronaut is not connected to the spacecraft—was made on February 1984 by Bruce McCandless. In 1991, on the very first flight of the Space Shuttle *Endeavor*, the program had another first—the first three-person spacewalk—when three crewmembers captured (and then repaired) a malfunctioning satellite.

INTERNATIONAL ASTRONAUTS

BECAUSE THE SPACE shuttle takes astronauts to the International Space Station, it has hosted crewmembers from around the globe. Belgium, Canada, France, Germany, Israel, Italy, Japan, Mexico, the Netherlands, Russia, Saudi Arabia, Spain, Sweden, Switzerland, and Ukraine have all sent astronauts into space on the shuttle!

Astronaut Bruce McCandless on his historic untethered spacewalk. On his back, McCandless wore a Manned Maneuvering Unit (MMU), a nitrogen-fueled jet pack.

The Space Shuttle *Atlantis* docking with the Russian Space Station *Mir* in July 1995. *Atlantis* was the first space shuttle to dock at the Russian space station.

THE SHUTTLES

BEFORE THE LOSS of *Challenger* in 1986 and *Columbia* in 2003, the original shuttle fleet included five orbiters:

- *Atlantis.* First flight: October 3, 1985.
- *Challenger.* First flight: April 4, 1983. (Lost on January 28, 1986)
- *Columbia.* First flight: April 12, 1981. (Lost on February 1, 2003)
- *Discovery.* First flight: August 30, 1984.
- *Endeavor.* First flight: May 7, 1992.

Space Tragedies

The business of exploring faraway places has always been a risky endeavor. Thousands lost their lives venturing westward across the Atlantic Ocean to America in search of lands beyond the horizon. Hundreds died climbing the world's tallest peaks before any was summited. And so it has been in the exploration of space.

The *Apollo 1* Fire

The first American deaths in the space program occurred on January 27, 1967. During a ground test for the *Apollo 1* mission, Gus Grissom, Ed White (1930–1967), and Roger Chaffee (1935–1967) were killed when fire engulfed their command module. Because the capsule's hatch opened inward and was sealed by several latches, the astronauts could not be rescued. As often occurs after a tragedy, those deaths instigated a number of changes in the capsule's design, including a hatch that could be easily opened from the outside.

The Crash of *Soyuz 1*

Cosmonaut Vladimir Komarov (1927–1967) was the first publicly acknowledged death in the Soviet space program, as well as the first in-flight space fatality. *Soyuz 1* was launched on April 23, 1967; its elaborate mission was to rendezvous with *Soyuz 2*, which was to be launched a day later. But the second launch was delayed, and *Soyuz 1* suffered multiple equipment malfunctions, the last of which was the failure of parachutes that would slow the capsule's impact as it returned to Earth. Komarov died on impact when *Soyuz 1* crash-landed on April 24, 1967.

From left, Gus Grissom, Ed White, and Roger Chaffee of *Apollo 1*. The fire that claimed the lives of the three men spread so quickly in part because the capsule was filled with pure oxygen, which is highly flammable.

Vladimir Komarov was the first Soviet to go into space more than once. His ashes are now entombed in the Kremlin Wall Necropolis in Moscow, Russia.

LATER AMERICAN DISASTERS

Space Shuttle _Challenger:_ For nearly 20 years after the _Apollo 1_ tragedy, the American space program was unmarred. That changed on January 28, 1986, when the Space Shuttle _Challenger_ broke apart 73 seconds after liftoff. The crew of seven—which included Christa McAuliffe (1948–1986), a social studies schoolteacher from New Hampshire—all died as the craft disintegrated.

Space Shuttle _Columbia:_ When the space shuttle _Columbia_ was launched on January 16, 2003, a piece of foam insulation broke off one of the fuel tanks and damaged the system that protected the craft from the heat of reentry. NASA knew that the foam had broken off, but did not know the extent of the damage. On February 1, as _Columbia_ reentered Earth's atmosphere, it disintegrated over Texas. All seven astronauts were lost.

Concord, New Hampshire teacher, Christa McAuliffe trains in zero-gravity conditions before the ill-fated _Challenger_ mission.

The six astronauts who lost their lives in the _Columbia_ disaster are memorialized on a plaque affixed to the Mars Spirit Rover. The plaque is mounted on the rover's antenna.

DEATH OF A LEGEND

HE WAS THE HERO of the Soviet space program and the world: Yuri Alexeyevich Gagarin. He took up flying as a hobby when he was a teenager, and in 1961 he became the first human in space and the first to orbit Earth. After his historic flight, Gagarin toured the world to promote the Russian space program. He then returned to his earlier life as a fighter pilot.

Yuri Gagarin died on March 27, 1968, during a routine training flight when the MiG-15UTI he was piloting crashed in Russia. The cause of that crash is still unknown, but to this day, Gagarin is still a hero in his country.

This statue of Yuri Gagarin, in the city of Lyubertsy, Russia—where Gagarin attended school—is just one of dozens of Russian monuments to the first human in space.

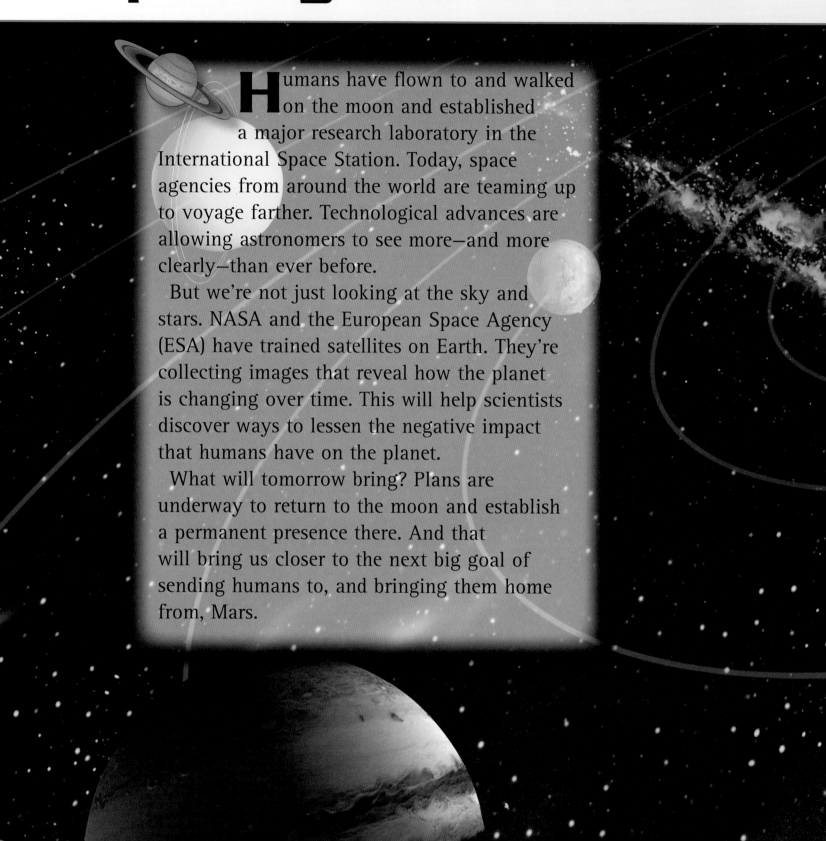

Humans have flown to and walked on the moon and established a major research laboratory in the International Space Station. Today, space agencies from around the world are teaming up to voyage farther. Technological advances are allowing astronomers to see more—and more clearly—than ever before.

But we're not just looking at the sky and stars. NASA and the European Space Agency (ESA) have trained satellites on Earth. They're collecting images that reveal how the planet is changing over time. This will help scientists discover ways to lessen the negative impact that humans have on the planet.

What will tomorrow bring? Plans are underway to return to the moon and establish a permanent presence there. And that will bring us closer to the next big goal of sending humans to, and bringing them home from, Mars.

Venus and Jupiter

This image of Venus, taken by *Magellan*, has been enhanced to show the planet's surface.

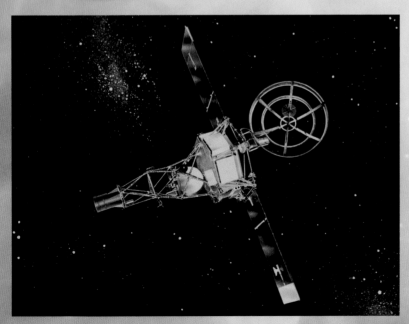

Sometimes called "Earth's sister planet" or "Earth's twin," Venus is much like Earth in some ways: its gravity, size, mass, and composition are very similar to those of our home planet. But Venus's surface temperature is blazingly hot, averaging 864°F. That's because the planet's thick, cloudy cover and atmosphere of carbon dioxide (the gas we exhale) traps in the sun's heat. And all that heat means that Venus is bone dry.

Jupiter is the largest planet in the solar system. Whereas Venus is much like Earth in its makeup, Jupiter is more like a star. In fact, it may have become a star if it had grown

This radar image, taken by *Magellan*, shows a 3D-view of the cratered surface of Venus.

larger. One of Jupiter's most impressive characteristics is the fact that the planet has its own moons—more than five dozen at last count!

What do these two planets have in common? They have both been extensively explored by unmanned space probes, and more missions are being planned today.

Exploring Venus

For many years, NASA and the USSR tried unsuccessfully to launch probes to Venus. In 1962, NASA's *Mariner 2* made the first successful flyby of the planet. More recently, the *Magellan* orbiter explored the planet. Launched from the space shuttle in 1989, *Magellan* collected data and mapped 98 percent of the planet's surface. The orbiter also revealed that most of Venus's surface is covered by volcanoes.

Launched in 2005 by the ESA, *Venus Express* is currently orbiting Venus. So far, it has detected a very rare molecule called hydroxyl and revealed massive weather patterns that affect the entire planet.

The Mariner space probe measured the solar winds that create the swirling clouds of Venus.

On to Jupiter

The first mission to Jupiter was a flyby by the spacecraft *Pioneer 10*. Launched in 1973 by NASA, *Pioneer 10* was the first craft to travel beyond the asteroid belt and observe the planet. As did the Venus probes, *Pioneer 10* sent back spectacular images of Jupiter. It also gathered information about the planet's moons, atmosphere, and interior.

Two missions to Jupiter are in the planning stages. In 2011, NASA will launch *Juno*, a solar-powered craft that will reach the planet five years later. Juno will gather information about Jupiter's atmosphere, its gravitational field, and its makeup, all of which will help scientists better understand how the planet formed.

Scheduled to launch in 2020 at the earliest, the *Europa Jupiter System Mission* will send two robotic orbiters to Jupiter, where they will gather data about the planet and then travel to two of its moons, Ganymede and Europa. NASA and the ESA are undertaking this mission.

THREE KINDS OF MISSIONS

THREE KINDS OF MISSIONS have visited the planets in our solar system: flybys, soft landings, and hard landings. Based on their names, you can probably figure out what they mean.

On a flyby, a probe or satellite simply passes by a planet, taking photographs and gathering information. A soft landing means that a probe actually lands on the planet's surface rather than crashing—which is another name for a hard landing.

Jupiter's famous red spot, above, is actually an enormous storm system almost three times the size of planet Earth. It's just one of the many mysteries of the planet that scientists hope to unlock.

Exploring Mars

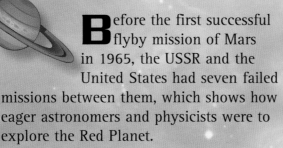

Before the first successful flyby mission of Mars in 1965, the USSR and the United States had seven failed missions between them, which shows how eager astronomers and physicists were to explore the Red Planet.

But NASA's *Mariner 4* succeeded and took the very first close-up pictures of Mars. Those images revealed a cratered, rust-colored surface that showed some evidence of flowing water.

The image below depicts an artist's rendering of what one of the Mars rovers might look like on the surface of the Red Planet. Each rover is equipped with a panoramic camera and instruments that allow it to analyze rocks.

DID YOU KNOW?

On March 31, 2009, a group of ESA and Russian astronauts in Moscow began a simulated mission to Mars. The six crew members entered a sealed "habitat" designed to replicate what a journey to the Red Planet might be like—from the launch and landing, to an exploration of the planet's surface, and complete with mock emergencies. They are slated to remain in the habitat for 520 days.

Earthly Elements

Thirty-six years later, on April 7, 2001, NASA launched the *2001 Mars Odyssey* orbiter. Among its findings was that the elements on Mars are very similar to those on Earth and that water was once found on the planet. Even though the orbiter's mission officially ended—as a resounding success—in 2004, the 2001 Mars *Odyssey* remains active today.

Red Planet Rovers

Currently, there are four active missions exploring Mars. The *Mars Express* orbiter (launched by the ESA in 2003) is searching for water beneath the planet's surface; the *Mars Reconnaissance* orbiter (launched by NASA in 2005) is looking for water and dust in Mars' atmosphere. Finally, the twin Mars Exploration Rovers—*Spirit* and *Opportunity*—which launched in 2003, are traveling the surface of the planet gathering evidence of past water from rocks, dust, and soil.

THE FUTURE OF MARS EXPLORATION

THREE MISSIONS TO MARS are currently in the works.

Mars Science Laboratory (MSL). This technologically advanced rover is a traveling lab that will drill into the Mars surface, scoop up soil and dust samples, and collect and analyze rocks. When NASA launches it in 2011, *MSL* will be the most complex and sophisticated piece of equipment on Mars.

Mars Scout 2. Also scheduled for a 2011 launch, the *Mars Scout 2* is one of a series of smaller NASA missions. The first Scout mission was the *Phoenix* lander, which confirmed that water and/or ice existed beneath the surface of Mars and sent more than 25,000 pictures of the planet back to Earth. *Mars Scout 2* could take the form of a balloon, a lander, or an orbiter: that decision will be based on the findings of missions already exploring the planet.

Maven. Set to launch by NASA in 2013, the *Mars Atmosphere and Volatile Evolution Mission,* or *MAVEN,* will orbit Mars' upper atmosphere looking for clues about the planet's climate and atmosphere—which used to be dense enough to support liquid water on the planet's surface.

The 2001 Mars *Odyssey* orbiter lifts off from Cape Canaveral, Florida.

The large dark spot on Mars' surface was once thought to be an enormous plain. We now know that it is, in fact, a huge volcano. The area is dark because it lacks the dust that covers most of the rest of the planet.

The solar system's largest canyon is on Mars. The Velles Marineris is an enormous valley that stretches for 1,864 miles—that's more than three times longer than our Grand Canyon.

Comets and Meteors

Go outside on a warm, clear night, spread out a blanket, lie down, and watch the sky. Relax and be patient, and you're sure to see tiny flashes of light blazing across the sky. Those flashes of light are really shooting stars, or meteors. Meteors are simply bits of outer space dust or rock that have entered the earth's atmosphere. The trail of light you see is the object burning up as it speeds through the sky. Before a bit of space rock or dust enters the earth's atmosphere, it's called a meteoroid. Billions of meteoroids are orbiting the sun right now, and many of them have come from comets.

Anatomy of a Comet

As we've learned, comets are balls of ice and rock that orbit the sun. As the comet gets closer to the sun, some of its ice melts and solar winds push the vapor and dust away from the comet's head, or nucleus and create its tail, which can be millions of miles long.

A few comets are visible when they come close to Earth, but they do not flash across the sky the way meteors do. Rather, they appear as fixed objects, like a planet. Astronomers classify comets in two ways: Long-period comets take more than 200 years to orbit the sun; short-period comets circle the sun in less than 200 years.

As meteors enter the earth's atmosphere, friction causes them to heat up and give off a bright glow. Millions of meteors approach Earth on a daily basis, but most burn up in the atmosphere before reaching land or ocean.

COMET CONTACT

NASA'S *DEEP IMPACT* space probe was designed to make physical contact with a comet (Tempel 1) back in 2005. After successfully completing that mission, during which it collected debris from the comet's interior, *Deep Impact* was renamed *EPOXI* and is now scheduled to study a second comet, Comet Hartley 2, in late 2010.

Another probe's mission has also been extended to visit Tempel 1. *Stardust* completed its mission to gather data about a comet called Wild 2 in 2007. It was renamed *NExT* and is slated to fly by Tempel 1 in early 2011.

Once it got within range of Tempel 1 (as seen in this illustration), the *Deep Impact* probe fired a projectile called an "impactor" to collide with the comet.

Comet Hale-Bopp, as photographed over California in 1997

FAMOUS COMETS

Comet Halley. This is perhaps the world's best-known comet. It comes close to Earth every 75 or 76 years. It last appeared in 1986 and will circle back near Earth again in mid-2061, when it will be visible with the naked eye.

Comet Kohoutek. This long-period comet was last visible from Earth in 1973; in fact, the crews of *Skylab 4* and *Soyuz 13* observed the comet. Don't wait up for its next appearance—it's not for 75,000 years.

Comet Hale-Bopp. Discovered in 1995, Hale-Bopp made a spectacular appearance in the night sky for 18 months starting in May 1996. By January 1997, it was visible from most everywhere, even cities. A long-period comet, it will not be visible from Earth until around 4380.

Halley's comet

European Space Agency

At the beginning of the space race in 1957 and for the next 20 years, the United States and Russia were the primary explorers of space. Conducting research, manufacturing space vehicles and equipment, training astronauts, planning missions, and launching rockets are all very expensive endeavors, and in the beginning, only the world's two "superpowers" were able to operate full-scale, independent space programs.

Group Effort

In 1975, the European Space Agency (ESA) was formed in Paris, France. It brought together smaller organizations from across Europe that were already conducting research and building and launching satellites. Belgium, Germany, Denmark, France, the United Kingdom, Italy, the Netherlands, Sweden, Switzerland, and Spain were the founding members. The ESA would allow member countries to pool their collective resources, enabling those countries to explore space on a level with the United States. Today, the ESA works with NASA on international projects.

Satellite Launches

The ESA's debut project was the launching of *Cos-B*, a satellite that monitored gamma rays, which are bursts of a very powerful type of radiation. Over the years, more countries joined the ESA, and the agency became important for launching commercial satellites—those owned by companies rather than governments.

The European Space Agency

- ESA member countries
- European cooperating states
- countries that have signed a cooperation agreement

ATLANTIC OCEAN

NORWAY

FINLAND

SWEDEN

ESTONIA

IRELAND

UNITED KINGDOM

E U R O P E

GERMANY

POLAND

BELGIUM

CZECH REPUBLIC

UKRAINE

FRANCE

SWITZERLAND

AUSTRIA

HUNGARY

SLOVENIA

ROMANIA

PORTUGAL

SPAIN

ITALY

Black Sea

TURKEY

GREECE

Mediterranean Sea

OTHER ESA MISSIONS

THE ESA ALSO DOES important work in space exploration. Here's the lowdown on four of its groundbreaking missions.

SOHO. In 1995, the ESA and NASA launched a space-based observatory called SOHO (SOlar Heliospheric Observatory) that gathered information about the sun. In fact, SOHO has provided more information about the sun than any other research.

Rosetta. This robotic spacecraft was launched in 2004 on a mission to study a comet called Churyumov-Gerasimenko, which orbits the sun every 6.6 years. Slated to reach the comet (named for the two men who discovered it) in 2014, *Rosetta* will be the first spacecraft to get a close-up look at a comet.

Herschel. When it is launched, probably in late 2009, Herschel will be the largest and most powerful infrared telescope in space. Herschel can see infrared light, a type of light that we cannot see with our eyes. That will allow astronomers to see through dust and learn about the origin and evolution of stars.

Planck. This observatory's job will be to study a type of radiation that will give astronomers important information about the origins of the universe. It is slated to be launched with Herschel in 2009.

This sunspot, as photographed by the SOHO spacecraft, is calculated to be almost 20 times larger than planet Earth.

Rosetta will send out a lander to touch down on comet Churyumov-Gerasimenko, as demonstrated in this illustration.

DID YOU KNOW?

The ESA trains its own astronauts: they are the members of the European Astronaut Corps (EAC), which was formed in 1998. It allows astronauts from many countries to receive standard training. EAC astronauts have participated in Russian and American missions to the International Space Station.

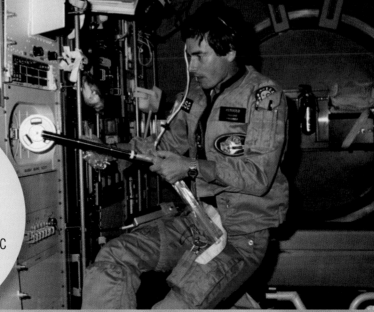

Seen here on the Space Shuttle *Columbia*, Ulf Merbold holds the distinction of being the first ESA astronaut in space.

Hubble and Webb

You've probably heard about the Hubble telescope. Named for astronomer Edwin Powell Hubble (1889–1953), Hubble made discoveries that helped develop a theory of how the universe was created. The solar-powered Hubble telescope orbits Earth every 97 minutes, collecting images of space that no land-based telescope could. Since it was launched in 1990, Hubble has beamed hundreds of thousands of images to Earth over the years.

What Have We Learned from Hubble?

Hubble's observations of distant galaxies—some as far as 108 million light-years from Earth!—helped scientists pinpoint the age of the universe to 13 to 14 billion years.

Images sent to Earth from Hubble of the Orion Nebula—a haze of gas and dust in the constellation Orion 1,500 light-years away—revealed how planets and stars can form in these swirling clouds. In 1994, the comet Shoemaker–Levy 9 collided with Jupiter. Hubble's amazing images of the impact provided astronomers with a close-up view of eight impact sites.

After Hubble, the Webb

The Hubble telescope was last serviced in 2008. It is now in the last stages of its lifespan. But a new telescope will soon take its place. In 2013, the James Webb Space Telescope (JWST), an orbiting infrared observatory, will be launched into space.

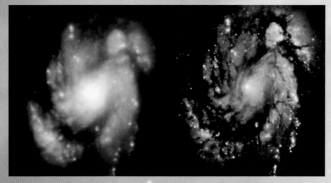

These images—of a galaxy called M100—shows Hubble's vision before and after it was fitted with a corrective lens.

CORRECTIVE LENS

AFTER THE HUBBLE was launched into orbit, scientists on Earth discovered that one of its mirrors was out of focus. To fix the problem, astronomers created a sort of contact lens for the telescope. The crew of Space Shuttle *Endeavor* took the lens with it into space, and repaired Hubble. And now the telescope has perfect vision!

In 2002, the crew of the Space Shuttle *Columbia* spent five days working on Hubble. The telescope received a new camera as well as some routine maintenance and upgrades. This is the view of the telescope from the shuttle on that mission.

With a mirror seven times larger than that of Hubble, the Webb—which is being built by NASA, the ESA, and the Canadian Space Agency—will allow astronomers to see even farther into space than Hubble.

Among the goals that astronomers have for the Webb are to look for the first objects formed after the universe was created, to find out how galaxies change as they age, and to find out whether life is possible in other solar systems.

HOW DOES IT WORK?

TELESCOPES ARE GIANT magnifying glasses, right? Wrong! Telescopes work by collecting more light than the human eye can detect. The bigger a telescope's mirror, the more light it can collect. Even though Hubble's mirror, at about 8 feet in diameter, is smaller than many Earth-based telescopes, it sees much farther because it is located above Earth's atmosphere.

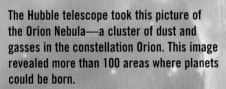

The Hubble telescope took this picture of the Orion Nebula—a cluster of dust and gasses in the constellation Orion. This image revealed more than 100 areas where planets could be born.

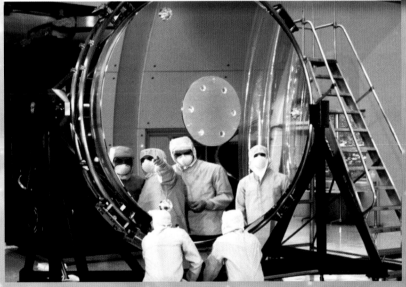

Scientists study Hubble's main mirror before its launch. All such work is done in "clean rooms," areas that are free of nearly all dust and other particles that could damage delicate instruments and equipment—which is also why these men and women are so well covered.

DID YOU KNOW?

Every week, Hubble sends about 120 gigabytes of data to Earth. That's about 30,000 songs, 150 hours of video, or 25,000 photographs worth of information!

The World in Space

Today, many countries around the world have a hand in the exploration of space. At last count, 51 countries—from Algeria to Vietnam—have their own space agency. What are these countries doing in space research? Many concentrate primarily on using research and technological advancements to aid their own economies. Some nations, India and Japan, for example, launch probes and operate satellites.

Mercury Mission

Collectively, space agencies around the world have sent probes and orbiters all around our solar system. The ESA and the Japanese Aerospace Exploration Agency (JAXA) are currently working together on a mission to Mercury called BepiColombo. Scheduled to launch in 2013, BepiColombo will send two orbiters to explore the closest planet to the sun. Those orbiters should reach their destination by 2019.

SPACE AGENCIES AROUND THE WORLD

HERE'S A LIST of all the countries that currently operate their own space agencies.

1. Algeria	18. India	35. Portugal
2. Australia	19. Indonesia	36. Romania
3. Austria	20. Iran	37. Russia
4. Azerbaijan	21. Israel	38. Saudi Arabia
5. Bangladesh	22. Italy	39. South Korea
6. Belgium	23. Japan	40. Spain
7. Brazil	24. Kazakhstan	41. Sweden
8. Canada	25. Malaysia	42. Switzerland
9. China	26. Mongolia	43. Taiwan
10. Colombia	27. Morocco	44. Thailand
11. Czech Republic	28. Netherlands	45. Tunisia
12. Denmark	29. Nigeria	46. Turkey
13. Ecuador	30. North Korea	47. Ukraine
14. France	31. Norway	48. United Kingdom
15. Germany	32. Pakistan	49. Uruguay
16. Greece	33. Peru	50. Venezuela
17. Hungary	34. Poland	51. Vietnam

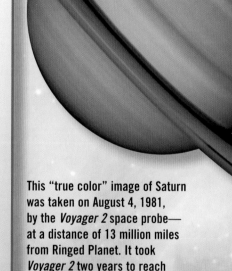

This "true color" image of Saturn was taken on August 4, 1981, by the *Voyager 2* space probe— at a distance of 13 million miles from Ringed Planet. It took *Voyager 2* two years to reach Saturn.

Our Solar System and Beyond

Both the United States and Russia have sent many orbiters and landers to Venus, and even more are planned. Jupiter and its moons have been the subjects of flyby missions and orbits, as have Saturn, Uranus, Neptune, and the dwarf planets Ceres and Pluto.

Some probes have left our solar system: *Voyager 1* and *Voyager 2*, both launched by NASA in 1977 are expected to send information about their interstellar travels back to Earth until 2020.

This is a full-scale model of the Voyager space probe; *Voyager 1* and *Voyager 2* are identical. Each is about the size and weight of a sub-compact car. But with a total mission cost of about $865 million, the two are far more expensive and complicated.

This photograph shows a NASA test that simulates space debris hitting a spacecraft or satellite. Here, a projectile is launched at 17,500 miles per hour at a solid surface. The resulting impact causes the burst of light, called an "energy flash."

SPACE JUNK

MORE COUNTRIES AND COMMERCIAL interests than ever before have access to space. According to the European Space Agency, the last 50 years of space exploration have launched 6,000 satellites into orbit. But only about 800 are currently in operation! And that's just satellites. There are approximately 12,000 additional objects—spent rocket stages, "garbage" from human missions, dead batteries, and at least one dropped tool bag—currently in low-Earth orbit. Depending on its altitude, that space debris could remain in orbit for hundreds, even thousands, of years.

This is a problem for existing satellites, shuttle missions, and the International Space Station, because all are at risk for damage caused by collisions with these objects. In early 2009, a U.S. satellite collided with a dead Russian satellite at about 22,000 miles per hour. The collision destroyed the U.S. satellite.

What's the solution for orbital debris? Creating less of it and moving what exists. Satellites could be commanded to return to Earth after a set period of time; spacecraft debris could be redirected to what's known as a graveyard orbit, an orbital path around the earth where satellites aren't usually launched.

What's Next?

What does the future of space exploration hold? Will humans return to the moon? Build colonies on Mars? Perhaps in the not-so-distant future people will be able to go on vacations to space.

Space Tourism

Today, civilian space travel, or space tourism, is something only the very rich can afford. For instance, in 2009, U.S. citizen Charles Simonyi paid $35 million for his *second* vacation aboard a Russian spacecraft. But now, Russia, which was the

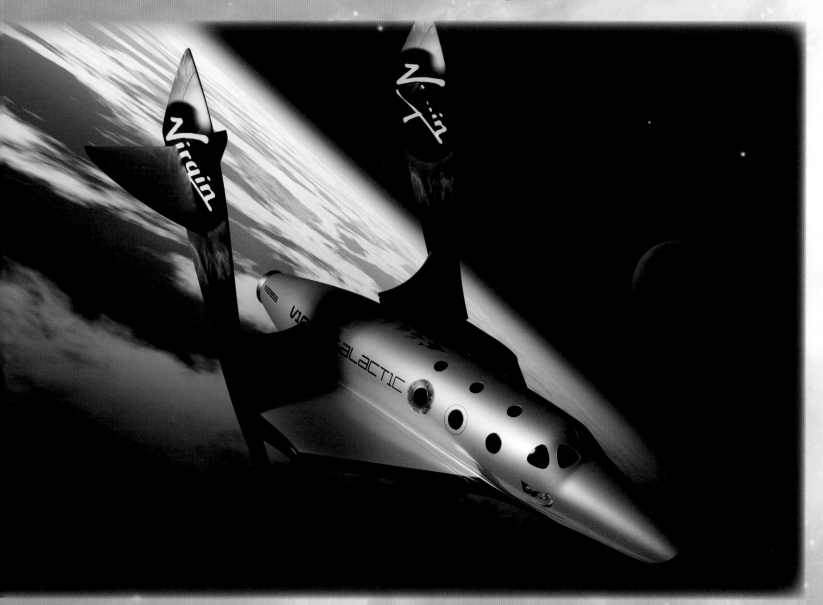

An artist's conception of *SpaceShipTwo*. If its program of suborbital flights proves to be successful, Virgin Galactic has plans to design *SpaceShipThree* for orbital trips.

only country offering flights to civilians, has discontinued trips for tourists because it is doubling the size of its space station crew, from three to six. That means private companies are beginning to step in to fill a demand that will certainly grow. Ready to book your flight? The world's first "spaceline"—Virgin Galactic—is selling seats for suborbital flights (flights into space that do not orbit Earth) at $200,000 a piece, but you can reserve yours for just $20,000, a bargain compared to what Simonyi paid. The spaceship is still in the design and production stages and no launch date has been set, but customers are already lining up for the trip.

Training for Space

NASA astronauts train for two years before they can fly into space. But Virgin Galactic customers will train for only three days before they embark on their 2½-hour journey to 70,000 feet aboard *SpaceShipTwo*. Much of the training will involve learning to cope with the giddiness, nausea, and weakness that astronauts often experience in microgravity. Space tourists will also have to pass a routine medical exam.

Wearing an official Russian spacesuit, U.S. citizen Charles Simonyi (left) poses for a picture with cosmonauts Oleg Kotov (center) and Fyodor Yurchikhin (right) during training for his space flight.

BACK TO THE FUTURE

THE NEXT BIG thing in government-sponsored space exploration will probably be a trip . . . back to the moon. That's right. NASA, in conjunction with 13 other space agencies, is working on a plan for return trips to the moon to "build a sustainable long-term human presence," and prepare for "future human and robotic missions to Mars and other destinations."

BYPRODUCTS OF EXPLORATION

ADVANCES IN SPACE EXPLORATION often yield much more than information about distant planets, moons, and stars. Many of the products we use in our everyday lives were invented or improved as a direct result of space research. Here are just a few.

Scratch-resistant lenses. If you wear glasses, you probably know that one of the available options for the lenses is a scratch-resistant coating. NASA developed that thin film.

Ear thermometer. Those instant-read thermometers that take your temperature by measuring the amount of infrared energy given off by the eardrum were developed by NASA's Jet Propulsion Lab in conjunction with a California company.

Protective sports equipment. Whether it's a batting helmet for a Little Leaguer or shoulder pads for an NFL player, most modern protective sports gear owes its effectiveness to Temper Foam, a padding originally designed to alleviate the impact of the G-forces experienced by astronauts during liftoff.

Find Out More

Words to Know

asteroid. A rocky object from a few feet to several hundred miles wide that orbits the sun

astrology. The study of the positions of the planets, stars, and other celestial bodies in the belief that they can affect human behavior

astronaut. A person who has been specially trained to travel in space

astronomy. The study of galaxies, planets, and stars

atmosphere. The gasses that surround a planet, star, or other celestial body

axis. The imaginary pole or straight line around which a planet, moon, or other body rotates

comet. A ball of ice and rock particles that travels around the sun. The comet's "tail" is produced by the ice that has melted and turned into gas.

constellation. Groups of stars that appear to form patterns in the sky and that have been given names

cosmonaut. The Russian word for "astronaut"

European Space Agency (ESA). An organization of several European countries that is dedicated to space exploration

Extra Vehicular Activity (EVA). Anything an astronaut does outside the spacecraft. That can include walking in space or walking on the moon.

flyby. A space or aircraft flight that passes close to a designated location for observation purposes

galaxy. A cluster of stars, gas, and dust held together by gravity

gravity. The natural and invisible force that attracts two objects

light-year. The distance light travels in one year, or 6 trillion miles

Low Earth Orbit (LEO). Area around the earth, 100 to 1,240 miles above the earth's surface. LEO is where most satellites orbit.

Milky Way. The galaxy in which our solar system is located

moon. A celestial body that travels around a planet

nova. A star that suddenly becomes much brighter. When it becomes a nova, a dim star can become very bright. *Novae* is the plural of *nova*.

orbit. The path that an object travels around another object. The planets in our solar system orbit the sun.

planet. An object that is larger than an asteroid and that orbits a star. Our solar system is home to eight planets.

reentry. The period during which a spacecraft passes throughout the earth's atmosphere after traveling in space

revolve/revolution. The action of a planet or other body orbiting an object. When a body has orbited once around an object, it has completed one revolution. Earth *revolves* around the sun but *rotates* on its axis.

rocket. A flying vehicle that propels a spacecraft (or satellite or other object) into space

rotate. Spin; the action of a planet or other object moving on its axis. Earth *rotates* on its axis and *revolves* around the sun.

satellite. An object—natural or man-made—that orbits another object

shrapnel. Metal pellets that are enclosed in a large shell casing. When the shell is shot from a large gun, it explodes and creates a shower of shrapnel.

solar system. The community of planets and other bodies that orbit a sun

star. Very large celestial bodies that are made of hot gasses. Our Sun is a star; it is the center of our solar system.

Web Sites to Visit

Amazing Space

http://amazing-space.stsci.edu/

Web site of the Education Group of the Space Telescope Science Institute; the site "uses the Hubble Space Telescope's discoveries to inspire and educate about the wonders of our universe."

HubbleSite

http://hubblesite.org/

Award-winning Web site of the Space Telescope

Science Institute and the home of NASA's Hubble Space telescope, "the renowned orbiting telescope whose discoveries have forever altered our knowledge of the universe."

NASA Kids' Club

http://www.nasa.gov/audience/forkids/kidsclub/flash/index.html

An official NASA site, where kids can explore space and the planets with Buzz Lightyear, complete puzzles, and enter contests.

NASA for Students

http://www.nasa.gov/audience/forstudents/index.html

An official NASA Web site and resource for students with homework help, NASA video clips, and information about careers at NASA.

Planet Quest

http://planetquest.jpl.nasa.gov/

Official Web site of NASA's Jet Propulsion Laboratory. Features resources for exploring the planets, learning about space exploration technology, and finding out about NASA missions.

SETI Institute

http://www.seti.org/Page.aspx?pid=1241

Web site of the Search for Extraterrestrial Intelligence (SETI) Center. The Center's mission is "to explore, understand and explain the origin, nature, and prevalence of life in the universe."

Space Day

http://www.spaceday.com/

Official Web site of the Space Day educational initiative. The first Friday of each May is Space Day, which promotes math, science, technology, and engineering education.

Space Today Online

http://www.spacetoday.org/

Space Today Online provides information about human activities in and about space—past, present, and future.

Books to Read

Aguilar, David A. *11 Planets: A New View of the Solar System.* Washington, D.C.: National Geographic, 2008.

Aguilar, David. *Planets, Stars, and Galaxies: A Visual Encyclopedia of Our Universe.* Washington, D.C.: National Geographic, 2007.

Carson, Mary Kay. *Exploring the Solar System: A History with 22 Activities.* Chicago Review Press, 2006.

Dickinson, Terence, and John Bianchi. *Exploring the Night Sky: The Equinox Astronomy Guide for Beginners.* Scarborough, Ont.: Camden House, 1987.

Driscoll, Michael, and Meredith Hamilton. *A Child's Introduction to the Night Sky: The Story of the Stars, Planets, and Constellations—and How You Can Find Them in the Sky.* New York: Black Dog & Leventhal, 2004.

Dunham, Montrew, and Meryl Henderson. *Neil Armstrong: Young Flyer.* New York: Simon & Schuster, 2001.

Garlick, Mark A. *Atlas of the Universe.* New York: Simon & Schuster, 2008.

Jackson, Ellen, and Nic Bishop. *Mysterious Universe: Supernovae, Dark Energy, and Black Holes.* Boston: Houghton Mifflin Books, 2008.

Panchyk, Richard. *Galileo for Kids: His Life and Ideas.* Chicago Review Press, 2005.

Scott, Carole. *Space Exploration.* New York: DK Publishing, 2000.

Sparrow, Giles. *Cosmic.* New York: DK Publishing, 2008.

Stars and Planets by DK Publishing. New York: DK Publishing, 2007.

Stevenson, Augusta. *Wilbur and Orville Wright: Young Fliers.* New York: Simon & Schuster, 1986.

Stone, Tanja Lee, and Margaret A. Weitekamp. *Almost Astronauts: 13 Women Who Dared to Dream.* Somerville, Mass.: Candlewick Press, 2009.

Thimmesh, Catherine. *Team Moon: How 400,000 People Landed Apollo 11 on the Moon.* Boston: Houghton Mifflin Books, 2006.

Index

Credits

Abbreviations Used

BSP = *Big Stock Photo*; JI = *JupiterImages*; NASA = *National Aeronautics and Space Administration*; PTG=*PhotosToGo*; PD = *Public Domain*; SS = *Shutterstock*; Wi = *Wikimedia*

l = left, *r* = right, *t* = top, *b* = bottom; *m* = middle

3 NASA **4** SS/William Attard McCarthy **6***bl* NASA **7***t* SS/Diego Barucco **7***tl* PTG **7***tr* SS/Cristi Matei **7***m* SS/Sebastian Kaulitzki **7***br* SS/Eric Gevaert **7***b* BSP/AlienCat **8** SS/Stephen Girimont **10** Wi **11** Joanne Flynn **12** NASA **14** Wi **15***tl* SS **15***tr* JI **15***b* Wi/Mkfairdpm **16** JI **18***tl* Wi/Sir William Congreve/PD **18***bl* NASA **18***br* SS/Michael Ransburg **18***tr* NASA **19***l* NASA **19***r* PTG **20***tl* NASA **21***b* SS/Samot **22***tl* NASA **22***br* NASA **23***l* NASA **23***r* Wi/NASA **24***t* NASA **24***b* NASA **25***tl* JI **25***tr* NASA **25***br* NASA **26***l* NASA **26***r* NASA **27***t* NASA **27***bl* NASA **27***br* NASA **28***l* NASA **28***m* NASA **28***r* NASA **29***t* NASA **29***b* NASA **30** NASA **31***t* NASA **31***b* NASA **32** NASA **33***t* NASA **33***b* NASA

34*l* NASA **34***r* NASA **35***t* NASA **35***b* NASA **36** NASA **37***t* NASA **37***br* NASA **37***bl* NASA **38***tl* NASA **38***br* NASA **39***t* NASA **39***b* NASA **40** NASA **41***l* NASA **41***r* Wi/George100 **42** NASA **43***tr* NASA **43***br* NASA **43***l* NASA **44***l* NASA **44***r* NASA **45***t* NASA **45***b* NASA **46***l* NASA **46***r* NASA **47***t* NASA **47***b* NASA **48***l* NASA **48***r* NASA **49***t* NASA **49***b* NASA **50***l* NASA **50***br* NASA **51***bl* NASA **51***tr* NASA **51***br* Wi/Yuriy Lapitskiy **52** SS/Jurgen Ziewe **54***tl* NASA **54***bl* NASA **54***tr* NASA/JPL **55** NASA/JPL **56** NASA/JPL **57***tr* NASA **57***bl* NASA **57***br* JI **58** SS/Sebastian Kaulitzki **59***tr* NASA **59***bl* NASA **59***br* JI **61***m* NASA **61***t* NASA **61***b* NASA **62***l* NASA **62***r* NASA **63***bl* NASA **63***tr* NASA **64** NASA **65***b* NASA **65***t* NASA **66** Wi/VirginGalactic **67** NASA **68***tl* SS/Torian **68***br* SS/Torian **69** SS/Torian

Elements JI

Backgrounds NASA

Cover NASA; JI; JI; JI; PTG